RECOVERY OF THE GOSPEL

BY

E. A. JOHNSTON

ISBN: 979-8-9921926-2-9

Printed in the United States of America

Formatting and Publishing by
The Old Paths Publications, Inc
11246 Oyster Bay Circle
New Port Richey, FL 34564
TOP@theoldpathspublications.com
www.theoldpathspublications.com
January 2025

COVER PHOTO:

Regarding the cover photo: The author is in the pulpit of St. Mary de Crypt, Gloucester, England, from which George Whitefield preached his first sermon and sent 15 people mad.

DEDICATION

The following study on the recovery of the Old Gospel is hereby dedicated to the memory of the mighty Canadian evangelist, Ernest W. Wakefield, who fearlessly preached the Old Gospel to a young, thirteen year-old-boy who attended a Revival Meeting and heard about the ruin of man, his duty of repentance, and his need of a bloodstained Saviour for Sin in the Person of Christ Jesus. And who came to Christ that fateful night in Oak Park, Illinois in the tumultuous year of 1968. All to the grace of the glory of God.

E.A. Johnston
January 2025

TABLE OF CONTENTS

DEDICATION 3

TABLE OF CONTENTS...5

INTRODUCTION 7

CHAPTER ONE: WHY IS RECOVERY NEEDED?.11

CHAPTER TWO: MUST BE PREACHED IN ITS PURITY AND PROPER ORDER 15

 THE TWO MESSAGES OF THE CROSS............ 17

 THE FIRST MESSAGE OF THE CROSS IS: GOD MUST PUNISH SIN.. 17

 THE SECOND MESSAGE OF THE CROSS IS: CHRIST THE SUBSTITUTE FOR SIN 22

CHAPTER THREE: GETTING MEN LOST 29

CHAPTER FOUR: THE FOUR R'S: 35

 RUIN.. 36

 REPENTANCE.. 38

 WE ARE NOT PREACHING THE GOSPEL IF WE ARE OMITTING REPENTANCE 39

 GOD COMMANDS ALL MEN TO REPENT........ 40

 REGENERATION 42

 YE MUST BE BORN AGAIN 42

 REDEMPTION 45

CHAPTER FIVE: A BLOODY CROSS.................**49**

CHAPTER SIX: THE LORDSHIP OF CHRIST.......**55**

CHAPTER SEVEN: AUTHORITY IN THE PULPIT .**61**

CHAPTER EIGHT: UNCTION: POWER IN THE PULPIT..**67**

CHAPTER NINE: THE LAST JUDGMENT **77**

CHAPTER TEN: SAMPLE SERMONS.................**83**

Gospel Sermon #1:.. 83

GOOD ENOUGH FOR HEAVEN AND NOT BAD ENOUGH FOR HELL 83

RELIGION WON'T SAVE YOU 86

YOU MUST BE BORN AGAIN 87

Gospel Sermon #2:.. 91

LIKE MUSTARD ON A BLUE SUIT 91

Gospel Sermon #3:.. 103

WITHOUT JESUS YOUR SINS WON'T SINK 103

FOUR PHOTOS **117**

ABOUT THE AUTHOR **121**

SOME OF THE BOOKS BY E. A. JOHNSTON ... 122

INTRODUCTION

The title of this work is "The Recovery of the Gospel"; the word "recovery" assumes that the object sought has been lost or misplaced or debased. This indeed is the case in our day of "Easy Believeism" where the modern evangelist has broadened the way of salvation in ways Jesus never did. Jesus said that few are saved and those who are saved with great difficulty; the way is narrow, the gate is straight, one must press through. Yet, the watered-down version of the gospel one hears today speaks of an easy way to heaven—all you have to do is believe. There is no mention of man's duty of repentance, no mention of man's utter necessity of regeneration. No talk of salvation being something that God does by performing a work of grace upon the heart. Rather, we have taken salvation out of the hands of God and placed it in the hands of men.

The author has been a student of revival for the last forty years. I have read and re-read sermons from the Great Awakening and the Second Great Awakening in America and noticed a vast dissimilarity between the content of the preaching of that day and our modern day. The Old Gospel that was preached in times of spiritual awakening was a God-centered Gospel of the doctrines of grace that produced reverence for Almighty God, heart-felt repentance toward a holy God, and deep humility on the part of the sinner in recognition of a beggar receiving undeserved mercy. The new Gospel of our day is a man-centered Gospel that elevates man. It shrinks God down to man's size and places the Creator on the same level as man. Man is now the author of his salvation and not God. Man decides. Man saves himself. This kind of man-centered Gospel is akin to mere humanism and this New Gospel centers on the happiness of man. Whereby the Old Gospel, the God-centered Gospel centered on the glory of God in the salvation of sinful man. This is why there is no fear of God in the land today nor behind our pulpits. Sin is rampant in and out of the church, which is antinomianism.

This dire situation is the reason why we need a recovery of the Gospel in our day. The Apostle Paul stated in Romans: "How then shall they call on him in whom they have not believed? and how shall they believe in him of whom they have not heard? and how shall they hear without a preacher" (Romans 10:14)?

We need preachers who will preach the God-centered gospel of our fathers that sparked revival and spiritual awakenings in former times. This book will provide that proper understanding of what is the unvarnished biblical gospel as compared to the debased variation we have today. May you read this book for your profit and the good of souls all to the glory of God!

CHAPTER ONE

WHY IS A RECOVERY OF THE GOSPEL NEEDED?

"Men today are more concerned about detailing their automobiles than they are concerned about the details of their eternal destiny."

E. A. Johnston

When something is lost it needs to be found. When something is missing there needs to be an awareness that something is missing. Regarding our modern gospel, men have rewritten it, debased it, and diluted it to make it more palatable to sinful man. All the hard sayings of Jesus are removed from the gospel of our day to where all the teeth of the gospel have been extracted to make it easier to gum down and digest. But does the gospel of our day resemble the biblical gospel of the Apostle Paul's day and the early church? Does the gospel of our day resemble the gospel of the Reformers? The Puritans? The Covenanters? Does the gospel of our day have any similarity to the God-centered gospel of Jonathan Edwards, George Whitefield, and Charles Spurgeon? Or is it the man-centered gospel of religious humanism? Is the real gospel even preached much anymore?

In the 17th century a wealthy Englishman traveled to Scotland in his carriage to hear good preaching. The first preacher he heard proclaimed the majesty and Sovereignty of a high and lifted God in all His glorious attributes, and his text was from Isaiah chapter six on the prophet Isaiah's vison of heaven where he states, *"I saw also the Lord sitting upon a throne, high and lifted up, and his train filled the temple"* (Isaiah 6:1); and upon hearing this he went away humbled by that vision of a holy God, high and lifted up. The next Scottish preacher he heard preached on the ruin of fallen man and the depravity of his heart because of man's ruined nature he had a poison in his blood and his text was from the Book of Job: *"How much more abominable and filthy is man, which drinketh iniquity like water"* (Job 15:16)? And upon hearing this he went away from the preaching humbled in his heart at how wicked and vile a sinner he really was; how guilty he was before a holy God! The last Scottish preacher he heard proclaimed the beauty of Christ Jesus as the Savior for sin and how powerfully this preacher held up Jesus as the only remedy and refuge for sin! His text was from Matthew's Gospel on the pearl of great price: *"Again the kingdom of heaven is like unto a merchant man seeking goodly pearls: who, when he had found one pearl of great price, went and sold all he had, and bought it"* (Matthew 13:45-46). The Englishman went away from that sermon with the picture of Jesus Christ precious as the Great Pearl of inestimable value, who was worth selling all for and losing all for so that He may be gained! On his journey back to England he contemplated all these powerful Biblical truths of the Gospel which he had heard while in Scotland. Finally, he had his carriage driver pull over near a forest, he got out and went into a grove of trees where he knelt on the ground and pondered in his heart those powerful gospel truths. Praying to God for mercy he confessed and repented of his sins and surrendered his heart to God and found salvation through faith in Christ Jesus. He returned to England a new man born from above and washed in the Blood! And the change was due to hearing sound doctrine of the Gospel of the Son of God preached to him under the power of the Holy Spirit!

As a revival scholar I have spent forty years in the study of historical revivals and spiritual awakenings. I have spent countless hours reading the sermons that were preached during the time period in America known as The Great Awakening and The Second Great Awakening. Upon reading those sermons I noticed a vast dissimilarity between what preachers were proclaiming in those times and what preachers are proclaiming in our times. Under the preaching of the gospel of those former days many souls were converted during glorious periods of revival that spread all over the nation. In our day very few are saved and fewer still preach the real gospel.

The diluted modern gospel of our day has no saving power for it is merely religious humanism. Rather, the gospel of the Apostle Paul had power to save, *"For I am not ashamed of the gospel of Christ: for it is the power of God unto salvation to every one that believeth; to the Jew first, and also to the Greek"* (Romans 1:16). There must be a "recovery" of that gospel. The one that "is the power of God unto salvation". Perhaps if we preachers began preaching the real biblical gospel again we would begin to see more conversions occur in our midst as the Holy Spirit once again attended our preaching of the gospel of the Son of God!

CHAPTER TWO

THE GOSPEL MUST BE PREACHED IN ITS PURITY AND PROPER ORDER

"Modern evangelism hands out Jesus like a free stick of chewing gum and folks take it and chew on it for a while until the flavor goes out of their religion."

E. A. Johnston

Today in our churches we offer people a Savior for sin before they even feel their need of a remedy for sin. If a man is in good health he feels no need for a physician, so Jesus told His hearers. *"When Jesus heard it, he said unto them, They that are whole have no need of the physician, but they that are sick; I came not to call the righteous, but sinners to repentance"* (Mark 2:17).

The gospel must be preached in its purity and proper order. This chapter will deal with the "proper order" of the gospel. Through preaching men must be brought to the place where they feel their need of a Savior for sin. We must first get men lost, before they can be saved. Asahel Nettleton, the primary leader of the Second Great Awakening, often preached that men could not be saved until they first became lost. We preachers today have forgotten that. Instead, we offer Jesus to a people who feel no need of Him, and they accept our little Jesus as a free ticket to heaven when they never believed they were guilty sinners on their way to Hell.

Our confusion today rests in the fact that we preachers do not properly understand what the real gospel is nor the order in which it needs to be preached. Look at Jesus in His dealings with the Samaritan woman at the well (John 4:7-31), there is much to be learned in how to present the gospel in its proper order in this biblical narrative. Notice that Jesus first confronts her with her sin: *"The woman saith unto him, Sir, give me this water, that I thirst not..."*(John 4:15). Here she is responding to the truth that Jesus has shared with her that He is the living water—but He does not offer Himself to her before He brings conviction of sin to her heart to have her feel her need of a Savior for sin. He tells her, *"Jesus saith unto her, Go, call thy husband, and come hither. The woman answered and said, I have no husband. Jesus said unto her, Thou hast well said, I have no husband. For thou hast had five husbands; and he whom thou now hast is not thy husband: in that, saidst thou truly"* (John 4:15-18). Upon hearing this the woman then responds, *"Sir, I perceive that thou art a prophet"* (John 4:19). This same woman soon is witnessing in her city about this Jesus who gave her "living water" and she is proclaiming *"Come, see a man, which told me all things that I ever did: is not this the Christ"* (John 4:29)*?* And she turns her city upside down for Christ!

But we evangelists today offer Jesus to people who feel no need of Him and they casually take Him like a free stick of chewing gum or a free ticket to heaven. Because of faulty evangelism our churches are full of the unconverted who never were awakened to their lost condition and need of a Savior for sin. I fear many today have believed that Jesus died for sin without ever believing on the Christ who died for sin.

THE TWO MESSAGES OF THE CROSS

If we are to preach the gospel in its proper order then we must learn the two messages of the cross and faithfully and boldly proclaim them.

THE FIRST MESSAGE OF THE CROSS IS: GOD MUST PUNISH SIN.

We must take a walk through our Bibles and read a running commentary of a continuous theme: GOD WILL PUNISH SIN.

"And God saw that the wickedness of man was great in the earth, and that

every imagination of the thoughts of his heart was only evil continually. And it repented the LORD that he had made man on the earth, and it grieved him at his heart. And the LORD said, I will destroy man whom I have created from the face of the earth" (Genesis 6:5-7).

We see from the lips of the Apostle Peter, that God is a God who must punish sin!

"For God spared not the angels that sinned, but cast them down to hell, and delivered them into chains of darkness, to be reserved unto judgment: And spared not the old world, but saved Noah the eight person, a preacher of righteousness, bringing in the flood upon the world of the ungodly: And turning the cities of Sodom and Gomorrah into ashes condemned them with an overthrow, making them an example unto those that after should live ungodly" (2 Peter 2:4-6).

And friends if you think God has changed His stripes as the God of the Old Testament and the God of the New Testament you are dead wrong!

"For I am the LORD, I change not" (Malachi 3:6).

Some folks think God is more tolerant toward sin these days but they fail to read their Bibles which declare GOD IS A GOD WHO WILL AND MUST PUNISH SIN!

> *"when the Lord Jesus shall be revealed from heaven with his mighty angels, in flaming fire taking vengeance on them that know not God, and that obey not the gospel of our Lord Jesus Christ: Who shall be punished with everlasting destruction from the presence of the Lord and from the glory of his power"* (Second Thessalonians 1:6-9).

A big reason why people are uninterested in the Gospel today and see no need for Jesus, is they are totally ignorant to the fact that God is a God who will punish sin. The trouble with our society today is that people sleep well at night because they don't believe God will punish sin. There is no fear of God in the land today and this blame can be placed on the pulpits of the land that quit preaching the undiluted Gospel of the Son of God. People don't believe God will punish sin. They do not believe in that kind of God. Even the majority of church members today do not believe in a God who will punish sin. Their God just wouldn't act that way. But listen, brother preacher, the God of the Bible will because the God of the Bible WILL AND MUST PUNISH SIN! When a church has poor theology, she doesn't act right. The main reason why many in our churches today (including ministers) tolerate sin in their lives is because they do not believe in a God who will punish sin. Therefore, Antinomianism is rampant throughout our churches today. People believe since they are "once saved, always saved" they can sin all they want to and still go to heaven! So you have a lot of church members who don't let their profession of faith interfere with their daily living because they refuse to believe in a God who would punish sin—especially theirs! We have turned God into a big jolly Santa Claus today who only exists to bless his little darlings. You can quote John 3:16 until you are blue in the face and nobody cares. We witness to the lost today with an anemic gospel message that has been so watered down it can't save a flea much less a hardened sinner; our witness falls on deaf ears because folks refuse to view God as a God who will punish sin. And no one will be interested in what Christ did on the cross until they believe that God will punish sin—meaning God will send them to Hell because of sin!

Consequently, we have forgotten what the message of the gospel is in your day and mine. Our little gospel message speaks only about "an offered Christ" who is stands helplessly at the door of the heart with his hat in his hand like an insurance salesman, who keeps knocking hoping you will let him in. This image of an impotent Christ is due to our man-centered gospel today that has taken salvation out of the hands of God and placed it in the hands of men. You decide if you want to be a Christian and you can do it anytime when you are good and ready.

Put it down big, plain and straight friend: there is no use to preach the second message of the cross, the forgiveness of sins through Christ's blood—because there is no use in offering a remedy for sin to people who don't feel their need of a remedy! This is why it is critically important to preach the first message of the Cross: THAT GOD IS A GOD WHO WILL PUNISH SIN. Then once folks realize they are in trouble, in danger, and they need a real remedy for their dirty, filthy, rotten sins, they will flee to Christ for refuge! Go study the sermons of the Puritans, or Jonathan Edwards, or Asahel Netttleton, men who were true to the true Gospel message, and who preached the Gospel in its purity and proper order.

This generation of hell bound sinners needs to hear the FIRST message of that bloody cross and that message is GOD WILL PUNISH SIN.

As those Roman soldiers nailed up the Son of God to that tree, as they fastened Him there with hammer and nails, every stroke of the hammer was an exclamation point crying out: GOD MUST PUNISH SIN! GOD MUST PUNISH SIN! GOD MUST PUNISH SIN!

> *"He that spared not his own Son, but delivered him up for us all, how shall he not with him also freely give us all things"* (Romans 8:32).

It is our job as preachers of the Gospel to preach it in its PROPER ORDER: THE FIRST MESSAGE OF THE CROSS IS: GOD WILL PUNISH SIN.

If we can get people today to admit that God is a God who must punish sin then maybe, just maybe they will listen to the second message of the cross:

THE SECOND MESSAGE OF THE CROSS IS: CHRIST THE SUBSTITUTE FOR SIN

You have to feel your need for a Savior from sin. Jesus is the pearl of great price worth selling all for and losing all for so He may be gained! Christ Jesus is the only remedy and refuge for sin. Man is a sinner in need of reconciliation to the God of the Bible who will by *"no means clear the guilty"* (Exodus 34:7). God must punish sin. Jesus spoke on this doctrine when He said: *"And fear not them which kill the body, but are not able to kill the soul:*

but rather fear him which is able to destroy both soul and body in hell" (Matthew 10:28).

If we are to preach the gospel in its proper order then the law must precede grace and men must know that God is a God who will and must punish sin, for the sentencing of the law will be carried out upon all guilty lawbreakers and rebels! Therefore, there is a need for pardon of sin in the Person of Christ Jesus, who shed His blood and died for our redemption, and He rose again and ascended back into heaven where He sits at the right hand of the Father and He earned that right by way of a bloody cross!

CHRIST DIED FOR SINNERS

"who loved me, and gave himself for me." (last phrase of Galatians 2:20).

The second message of the Cross is about that substitute who hangs there in my stead. Christ is God's sacrifice and my sin substitute. I have forgiveness of sins through Christ's blood. Jesus is the cure, the remedy for sin. The second message of the Cross is a lifting up of Christ Jesus as the Savior for sin.

A young Charles Spurgeon was converted to Christ when he heard a simple man preach a simple message of Christ on the Cross as a substitute for sin. His text was from Isaiah:

"Look unto Me, and be ye saved, all the ends of the earth, for I am God, and there is none else" (Isaiah 45:22).

Charles Spurgeon said, "I looked and saw that bleeding One on the Cross and looked and looked and looked, until I looked my eyes away."

We can present an "offered Christ" after we preach the first message of the Cross, then sinners will be hungry, weary thirsty for relief. The Gospel is for the hungry, the weary, and the thirsty. We must make sinners thirsty for Christ Jesus by preaching Christ and Him crucified!

> *"He is despised and rejected of men; a man of sorrows, and acquainted with grief: and we hid as it were our faces from him; he was despised and we esteemed him not. Surely he hath borne our griefs, and carried our sorrows; yet we did esteem him stricken, smitten of God, and afflicted. But he was wounded for our transgressions, he was bruised for our iniquities: the chastisement of our peace was upon him; and with his stripes we are healed. All we like sheep have gone astray; we have turned every one to his own way; and the LORD hath laid on him the iniquity of us all.*

"He was oppressed, and he was afflicted, yet he opened not his mouth: he is brought as a lamb to the slaughter, and as a sheep before her shearers is dumb, so he openeth not his mouth. He was taken from prison and from judgment: and who shall declare his generation? for he was cut off out of the land of the living: for the transgression of my people was he stricken. And he made his grave with the wicked, and with the rich in his death: because he had done no violence, neither was any deceit in his mouth. Yet it pleased the LORD to bruise him; he hath put him to grief: when thou shalt make his soul an offering for sin, he shall see his seed, and he shall prolong his days, and the pleasure of the LORD shall prosper in his hand. He shall see of the travail of his soul, and shall be satisfied: by his knowledge shall my righteous servant justify many, for he shall bear their iniquities" (Isaiah 53:3-11).

I challenge you friend, to go through the Book of Acts and see how the disciples preached and what message they preached. They would hold up a crucified Christ and point sinners to a bloodstained Savior for sin. The Second Message of the Cross: an offered Christ as the sinner's substitute is Good News to sinful man! But it is only good news when it is received and it won't be received until people hear the First Message of the Cross about a God of justice WHO WILL AND MUST PUNISH SIN. But in His mercy He has provided a remedy for sin in the Person of Christ Jesus.

> *"Then the soldiers of the governor took Jesus into the common hall, and gathered unto him the whole band of soldiers. And they stripped him, and put on him a scarlet robe. And when they had plaited a crown of thorns, they put it upon his head, and a reed in his right hand: and they bowed the knee before him, and mocked him, saying, Hail, King of the Jews! And they spit upon him, and took the reed, and smote him on the head. And after that that they had mocked him, they took the robe off from him, and put his own raiment on him, and led him away to crucify him"* (Matthew 27:27-31).

This is the message of the Gospel: Jesus came down here so we can go up there: He went about doing good, healing the sick, giving sight to the blind, even raising the dead to life. Yet He was taken by cruel hands and led to a place called Calvary where He was crucified. There, He suffered, died, and was buried. On the third day He rose again and appeared unto many: He then ascended back into heaven where He now sits at the right hand of the Father—and He earned that right BY WAY OF A BLOODY CROSS!

In John 14:6 Jesus says,

"I am the way, the truth, and the life; no man cometh unto the Father but by me."

Here Jesus answers the three greatest questions of the human heart.

"How can I be saved?"

Jesus said, *"I am the way."*

"How can I be sure?"

Jesus said, *"I am the truth."*

"How can I be satisfied?"

Jesus said, *"I am the life."*

And in John 6:35 Jesus declared:

"I am the bread of life: he that cometh to me shall never hunger, and he that believeth on me shall never thirst."

The Gospel is for the hungry, the weary, and the thirsty. Let me ask you friend: Are you hungry for God? Are you sick and tired of your sins? Are you thirsty for Christ? Then come to Him and believe on

Him and own Him as your Savior and Lord. The duty required is to come to Christ. And He has a pure Gospel promise to all who come: *"and him that cometh to me I will in no wise cast out"* (v. 37).

The First Message of the Cross is: GOD WILL PUNISH SIN

The Second Message of the Cross is: GOD HAS PROVIDED A REMEDY FOR SIN IN THE PERSON OF CHRIST JESUS!

As faithful ministers of the Gospel we must preach the Gospel in its purity and proper order.

We must not offer Jesus to folks until they feel their need of Him. We must be adept at getting men lost and this is the topic of our next discussion.

CHAPTER THREE
GETTING MEN LOST

"Today we fill our churches with the unconverted who merely made an 'intellectual ascent' to Jesus, and they claim to be saved but they have never been lost."

E. A. Johnston

Jesus told his hearers:

"For the Son of man is come to seek and to save that which was lost" (Luke 19:10).

The gospel must be preached in its purity and proper order and we will further discuss what that "proper order" entails. Men must be held up to the strictness and severity of God's unbending law. For a day will come when God will drop the plumbline of His holy law alongside men at the Final Judgement and all will fail that test, for

"all have sinned and come short of the glory of God" (Romans 3:23).

But we today fail to preach the law before grace. Both John Wesley and George Whitefield preached the law before grace; they believed that men must realize their guilt in sin before God and that they have transgressed God's holy law and therefore are under the condemnation for sin and the sentencing of the law must be carried out upon all guilty sin breakers! George Whitefield understood this clearly when he often stated, "A sinner must first be brought to Mt. Sinai before he can be brought to Mt. Zion."

Like Jesus dealing with the Samaritan woman at the well, we must bring sinners to feel conviction of sin—this is done through the preaching of man's duty of repentance. Men must be awakened to their lost condition and their perilous position of dying in their sins outside the blood of Christ. Our preaching should bring conviction of sin by the Holy Spirit. We must preach the law before grace and speak of the severity and strictness of God's unbending law that is the measure of men's guilt in sin. For sin is the transgression of the law:

> *"Whoseover committeth sin transgresseth also the law: for sin is the transgression of the law"* (1 John 3:4).

We find the Apostle Paul declaring the same sentiments about the law as the Apostle John, for in Romans we read,

> *"What shall we say then? Is the law sin? God forbid. Nay, I had not known sin, but by the law: for I had not known lust, except the law had said, Thou shalt not covet"* (Romans 6:7).

Our goal as preachers of the Gospel of the Son of God should be to preach doctrinally sound sermons on the full counsel of God. We must preach "searching sermons" that bring conviction of sin and the disturbing presence of Christ Jesus. We must use the Word of God to preach clearly that man is born with a ruined nature and a bent toward sin. In his natural condition he is under the condemnation of a holy God who must punish sin in a terrible region of misery called Hell. We must preach about the dangers of damnation in a devil's Hell. We must not be afraid of men like most preachers are today who only deliver nice little messages that don't disturb anyone—the problem is they don't save anyone either!

Getting men lost is our first objective in preaching the gospel: we must preach sound doctrine that awakens men to their lost condition to where they recognize their perilous position outside the blood of Christ Jesus. Once we get men lost, then the Holy Spirit can work upon their hearts bringing conviction of sin to where they see a "revealed Christ" so they can believe on Him. One is saved by receiving a revealed Christ who is now hidden in the bosom of the Father. *"No man hath seen God at any time; the only begotten Son, which is in the bosom of the Father, he hath declared him"* (John 1:18).

In the Book of Jeremiah we read:

"Is not my word like as a fire? saith the LORD; and like a hammer that breaks the rock in pieces" (Jeremiah 23:29)?

We must ask ourselves: What does a fire do? It awakens and alarms. If you are asleep in your home and the smoke alarms go off and you see flames and smell smoke, you are quickly awakened and alarmed at your danger and you rush to get your family out to safety. The gospel should be preached like a fire that awakens one to their lost condition and alarms them to seek a Savior for sin. God's Word is also described in Jeremiah as a hammer that breaks the rock in pieces. We should use the Word of God like a hammer to bust up every false foundation of carnal security and break apart every empty religious profession and the Gospel should smoke out sinners from their false refuges and bring them to Christ Jesus for salvation from sin.

When we preach with an objective to get men lost then we are preaching right and it is by this kind of preaching that the Holy Spirit can go to work on a sinner's heart. We must preach searching sermons that probe all the dark recesses of a sinner's heart.

A classic study in this is to read Jonathan Edwards sermon: "Sinners in the Hands of an Angry God." In Enfield, Connecticut on July 8th, 1741 Jonathan Edwards preached this now famous sermon where an eyewitness recorded in his diary: "We went over to Enfield where we met dear Mr. Edwards of Northhampton who preached a most awakening sermon from these words, Duet 32:35

> *'To me belongeth vengeance, and recompense; their foot shall slide in due time: for the day of their calamity is at hand, and the things that shall come upon them make haste'. And before sermon was done---there was a great moaning and crying out through ye whole house—What shall I do to be saved—Oh I am going to Hell—Oh what shall I do for Christ? to where the minister was obliged to desist from preaching –ye shrieks and cries were piercing and amazing."*[1]

---

[1] Oliver Means, "A Sketch of the Strict Congregational Church of Enfield, Conn.," (Hartford: 1899), p 192.

CHAPTER FOUR:

THE FOUR R'S: RUIN, REDEMPTION, REPENTANCE, REGENERATION.

"Men like Whitefield, Edwards, Spurgeon, and more recently, Lloyd-Jones, carried with them both a compass and barometer; the doctrines of grace were the compass; the felt presence of God in their lives was the barometer. Thus, they sailed on an even keel of theology and practice."

E. A. Johnston

In Acts, the Apostle Paul states,

"For I have not shunned to declare unto you all the counsel of God" (Acts 20:27).

Paul preached the hard sayings of the gospel: ruin, redemption, repentance, regeneration. But we today don't do that. We today don't want to offend our deacons or our wealthier members so we water down the gospel to make it more palatable to sinful man so he can swallow it easier without it being an offence to him. We modern evangelists preach an inoffensive gospel that has no power to save. But the gospel is an offence! We read the words of the Apostle Paul, *"For the preaching of the cross is to them that perish foolishness; but unto us which are saved it is the power of God"* (I Corinthians 1:18). We no longer preach the scandal of the Cross! To be crucified was a bloody spectacle and scandal in society!

RUIN

In preaching the Gospel of the Son of God, the Gospel of the grace of God, the Gospel of the Cross of God, must begin with the stark reality that man is a sinner who cannot save himself. Men need to know that God declares: *"Behold, all souls are mine; as the soul of the father, so also the soul of the son is mine; the soul that sinneth it shall die"* (Ezekiel 18:4).

We must begin with Ruin. Fallen man in Adam is born with a ruined nature and a bent toward sin. All men are sinners, *"For all have sinned, and come short of the glory of God"* (Romans 3:23). And the Bible describes the condition of man in his natural estate as the following: *"How much more abominable and filthy is man, which drinketh iniquity like water"* (Job 15:16), meaning, that man cannot get enough of sin! He drinks it down like water and is immediately thirsty for more! When presenting the Gospel to fallen man we preachers must begin with Ruin—man must see that he is a sinner. Man must admit that he is a rebel who stands against God in enmity to Him,

> *"Because the carnal mind is enmity against God: for it is not subject to the law of God, neither indeed can be"* (Romans 8:7).

Man must see clearly that as a sinner he stands under the condemnation of God,

> *"He that believeth on him is not condemned; but he that believeth not is condemned already, because he hath not believed in the name of the only begotten Son of God"* (John 3:18),

and the only remedy for sin is in the Person of the Lord Jesus Christ— *"There is therefore now no condemnation to them which are in Christ Jesus, who walk not after the flesh, but after the Spirit"* (Romans 8:1).

So the Gospel must be preached in its proper order. Man must see that he is a sinner in need of a Savior and man as a sinner must "feel" his need of a Savior for sin, before he is willing to come to Him for pardon of sin. We cannot offer Jesus as a "free ticket to heaven" to men and women and boys and girls who feel no need of a remedy for sin. This produces spurious conversions and fills our churches with baptized unconverted individuals who are religious but lost. One of the most dangerous persons in the world is a lost religious person (look at what the Pharisees and Scribes did to Christ the Son of God—they crucified the Lord of glory). Therefore, it is imperative when we preach the Gospel to begin with man's ruin; that man is a sinner with a poison in his blood and he needs a remedy for sin in the Person of Christ Jesus. This emphasis must be preached heavy and hard until our hearers actually come under conviction for sin that they indeed are guilty sinners on their way to Hell and that they deserve to go there!

REPENTANCE

The modern gospel of the last eighty years has placed an emphasis on God's love to the omission of His justice. Lewis Sperry Chafer (theology professor and founder of Dallas Theological Seminary) in his four volume "Systematic Theology" taught that repentance was not a necessary element to salvation. This was the Devil's seed that spurned the Easy Believe Gospel that took over the pulpits of the land and diluted the Old Gospel to make it more palatable to sinful man, and to make it easier to swallow. All you have to do to be saved is to "believe." So we have had modern evangelists widen the way of salvation in ways Jesus never did. Jesus said salvation was a strait gate that one had to press through and it was found along a narrow way and few were saved. Many are on the broad way that leads to destruction (Matthew chapter seven).

WE ARE NOT PREACHING THE GOSPEL IF WE ARE OMITTING REPENTANCE

Listen friend, unless you repent you will surely go to Hell even if you are the chairman of the deacons! Therefore, as preachers of the Old Gospel, the God-centered Gospel of the Cross, we must place a great deal of emphasis on that which Jesus placed a great deal of emphasis. Jesus said,

> *"I tell you, Nay: but, except ye repent, ye shall all likewise perish"* (Luke 13:3).

The Gospel is repent! Jesus began His earthly ministry by preaching REPENTANCE.

> *"Now after that John was put in prison, Jesus came into Galilee, preaching the gospel of the kingdom of God, and saying, The time is fulfilled, and the kingdom of God is at hand, repent ye, and believe the gospel"* (Mark 1:14-15).

The disciples of Jesus preached REPENTANCE.

> *"And they went out and preached that men should repent"* (Mark 6:12).

The resurrected Christ preached REPENTANCE.

After His resurrection from the dead, Jesus commanded His followers:

"Repentance and remission of sins should be preached in his name" (Luke 24:47).

The Apostle Paul preached REPENTANCE.

"Testifying both to the Jews, and also to the Greeks, repentance toward God and faith toward our Lord Jesus Christ" (Acts 20:21).

GOD COMMANDS ALL MEN TO REPENT

"And the times of this ignorance God winked at; but now commandeth all men every where to repent" (Acts 17:30).

THE EARLY CHURCH PREACHED REPENTANCE

"Then Peter said unto them, Repent, and be baptized every one of you in the name of Jesus Christ for the remission of sins, and ye shall receive the gift of the Holy Ghost" (Acts 2:38).

"The Lord is not slack concerning his promise, as some men count slackness; but is longsuffering to

usward, not willing that any should perish, but that all should come to repentance" (2 Peter 3:9).

"If we say that we have no sin, we deceive ourselves, and the truth is not in us" (1 John 1:8).

Brother preacher, how in the world can you claim to preach the Gospel if you omit man's duty of repentance and warn the wicked to flee from the wrath to come? This is a very solemn thing which you will face at the Judgment as you stand there with bloody hands:

"Son of man, I have made thee a watchman over the house of Israel: therefore hear the word at my mouth, and give them warning from me. When I say unto the wicked, Thou shalt surely die; and thou givest him not warning, nor speakest to warn the wicked from his wicked way, to save his life; the same wicked man shall die in his iniquity: but his blood will I require at thine hand. Yet if thou warn the wicked, and he turn not from his wickedness, nor from his wicked way, he shall die in his iniquity; but thou hast delivered thy soul" (Ezekiel 3:17-19).

A recovery of the Gospel must recover the missing doctrine of repentance to the lost and perishing!

REGENERATION

The Gospel of the glory of God must preach man's utter necessity of regeneration! Let me ask you a question friend: "Is man saved by a decision he makes? or by the regenerating work of the Holy Spirit?"

YE MUST BE BORN AGAIN

"There was a man of the Pharisees, named Nicodemus, a ruler of the Jews: the same came to Jesus by night, and said unto him, Rabbi, we know that thou art a teacher come from God: for no man can do these miracles that thou doest, except God be with him. Jesus answered and said unto him, Verily, verily, I say unto thee, Except a man be born again, he cannot see the kingdom of God. Nicodemus saith unto him, How can a man be born when he is old? can he enter the second time unto his mother's womb, and be born? Jesus answered, Verily, verily, I say unto thee, Except a man be born of water and of the Spirit, he cannot enter into the kingdom of God. That which is

born of the flesh is flesh; and that which is born of the Spirit is spirit. Marvel not that I said unto thee, Ye must be born again. The wind bloweth where it listeth, and thou hearest the sound thereof, but canst not tell whence it cometh, and whither it goeth: so is every one that is born of the Spirit" (John 3:1-8).

George Whitefield, the great British evangelist was a lost religious person when he was a student and a member of John Wesley's Holy Club at Oxford. He prayed, he read his bible, he gave alms, he fasted, he denied himself decent food and warm clothing, he visited the widows and orphans but he was still a lost religious man. Then, his good friend, Charles Wesley, loaned him a book written by a Scotsman named Henry Scougal. The book was *"The Life of God in the Soul of Man."* As a youthful George Whitefield read that book he realized, though a religious man, he was not a saved man; he did not have the "life of God in the soul of man" which meant the need to be born again. After Whitefield's conversion, he shook two continents for God in revival preaching the theme: "Ye must be born again!" After preaching to 20,000 hearers on Boston Common in 1740, a minister approached him and asked, "Mister Whitefield, you preach one sermon—Ye must be born again. When Sir, will you preach us another message?" to which the great evangelist replied, "When ye are born again!"

I fear many in our churches today only possess a mere intellectual ascent of Jesus—they are yet dead in sin, though religious. They need to have a work of grace wrought upon the heart by the supernatural work of the Spirit of God in regeneration. We need to warn men and women and boys and girls that they need regenerated hearts. Only God saves. If you are a saved individual friend, it is because God gave you saving faith.

> *"For it is by grace are ye saved through faith; and that not of yourselves; it is the gift of God: not of works, lest any man should boast"* (Ephesians 2:8,9).

The New Gospel has taken salvation out of the hands of God and placed it in the hands of men. You save yourself. But only God is the author of salvation for *"salvation is of the Lord"* (Jonah 2:9). It is God who works a work of grace upon the heart:

> *"A new heart also will I give you, and a new spirit will I put within you: and I will take away the stony heart out of your flesh, and I will give you an heart of flesh"* (Ezekiel 36:26).

Many revivals in history began when the ministers began to preach the doctrine of regeneration to their hearers. Brother preacher, are you preaching that today? Or are you more afraid of offending your unregenerate deacons? Ye must be Born Again!

REDEMPTION

Christ's work on the Cross, where He suffered, bled, and died for sinners like you and me is best explained by the following illustration. Years ago, when I was a younger man, I visited the ancient city of Ephesus in modern day Turkey. While there I was astonished by the remarkable reconstruction of those ancient ruins of a city of commerce and religion and the ministry of both the Apostle Paul (Paul caused a riot in the amphitheater, where 30,000 Ephesians gathered to cry with a loud voice, "Great is Diana") and the Apostle John (it is said he wrote the Gospel of John while living in Ephesus). I visited his tomb at the Church of St. John where tradition has it, he is buried.

While I was taking a guided tour of the ancient ruins of Ephesus, I was brought to a place along the main road which at the time was an agora. An agora in ancient times was a marketplace where items were bought and sold. Even, slaves were purchased in that marketplace called the agora. One of the Greek words for the word redemption is the word "agorazzo" which has the word "agora" in it. Regarding redemption, "agorazzo" means that

Christ entered the marketplace of sin and purchased me by His death and with His blood. He redeemed me for a price, and the price was His precious blood! There is another Greek word for redemption which employs the preposition "ek" which means to take out of. If you place the little Greek preposition, "ek" in front of the word "agorazzo" you get the word for redemption, "ek-agorazzo" which means: Christ not only entered the marketplace of sin and purchased me with His blood but He also brought me up and out of that marketplace of sin. Christ saves from the penalty of sin as well as from the power of sin!

But to better understand Christ's work on the Cross in our redemption we must look at the following verses of Scripture:

> *"According as he hath chosen us in him before the foundation of the world, that we should be holy and without blame before him in love; having predestined us unto the adoption of children by Jesus Christ to himself, according to the good pleasure of his will, to the praise of the glory of his grace, wherein he hath made us accepted in the beloved. In whom we have redemption through his blood, the forgiveness of sins, according to*

the riches of his grace" (Ephesians 1:4-7).

"Who hath saved us, and called us with a holy calling, not according to our works, but according to his own purpose and grace, which was given us in Christ Jesus before the world began" (2 Timothy 1:9).

Failure to recognize our true relationship to the death of our Lord Jesus Christ will hinder a proper understanding of the work of redemption. One must have a clear understanding of the biblical doctrine of the Covenant of grace to better grasp of Christ's work on the Cross whereby before the very foundation of the world, a Covenant was made between the Father and the Son and it was this: the Fall of Adam and all the consequences of sin in the Fall, God the Father gave unto His Son certain people out of humanity to be redeemed and rescued and the Son came into the world to do that very thing—to be a ransom for many. In the Gospel of John in chapter seventeen, we find Christ's priestly prayer in the shadow of the Cross and it is a wonderful exposition of this Covenant, *"As thou hast given him power over all flesh, that he should give eternal life to as many as thou hast given him"* (John 17:2). God's election is a free Sovereign, unconditional choice of sinners to be redeemed by Christ, given faith and brought to glory. The

Covenant of Grace is comprised of the three great acts of the holy Trinity in the recovery of lost mankind by election by the Father, redemption by the Son, calling by the Spirit (whereby the Spirit of God attends the Word of God in conviction and regeneration).

This understanding of Christ's redemptive work on the Cross should be a clarion call to evangelism not a hindrance to it (as in hyper-Calvinism). The Old Gospel, the God-centered Gospel is about a God who saves. Unfortunately, the New Gospel or man-centered Gospel of our day shrinks God down to man's size and takes salvation out of the hands of God and places it in the hands of men—you save yourself. The man-centered Gospel is to be helpful to man for his happiness. This New Gospel produces spurious conversions and false hope. The Old God-centered Gospel is the glory of God in the salvation of sinners. It is a proclamation of Divine sovereignty in mercy and judgment and it humbles man before a thrice holy God. The man-centered Gospel of our day elevates man—to the point of humanism!

We must have a recovery of the Old Gospel of the Son of God which is a God-centered Gospel that glorifies God in the salvation of sinners and encourages evangelism.

CHAPTER FIVE
A BLOODY CROSS

"We preachers today have gotten out our mop buckets and have cleaned up all the blood and gore around Calvary to make it so pristine you can sit and have your lunch there."

E. A. Johnston

Most preachers today just give nice little messages that don't offend anybody—the problem is they don't save anybody either! We preachers today have removed all the offensiveness and scandal of Calvary. A roman crucifixion was a public scandal! It was the most offensive and most painful form of execution. First, the criminal would be tormented by scourging. A Roman Flagrum was designed to quickly remove the flesh from the body of victim. The instrument was a short whip made of two or three leather thongs or ropes connected to a handle. The leather thongs were knotted with a number of small pieces of metal or broken glass designed to cut the skin of a victim. After a typical scourging the victim would have deep lacerations, torn flesh, exposed muscles and excessive bleeding which most of the time a scourging would leave a victim "half dead". Then he was brought bound in chains to a public subjugation on the cross, where he was stripped naked and nailed to a tree, fastened by nails pierced through the hands and feet.

A crucifixion would have many negative effects on the body including: interference with respiration—breathing would become difficult. A fluid build-up: fluid would build up around the heart and lungs which could cause the lungs to collapse and the heart to fail. Dehydration: one who was crucified would become dehydrated which could lead to hypovolemic shock. Pain: crucified victims experienced excruciating pain. Bleeding: one who was crucified would lose a lot of blood. The cross on which they died would be stained all with blood. Blood spatters would be on the ground beneath the cross.

We preachers today don't make mention of the ugliness and brutality of a Roman crucifixion. It was an inhuman form of execution carried out by barbarians. The spectacle of one crucified would draw a crowd much like public hangings used to draw crowds of spectators. A public crucifixion involved pain, shame, and ignominy—deep personal humiliation and disgrace. It was a scandal to be crucified.

"For Christ sent me not to baptize, but to preach the gospel: not with wisdom of words, lest the cross of Christ

should be made of none effect. For the preaching of the cross is to them that perish foolishness; but unto us which are saved it is the power of God" (1 Corinthians 17-18).

Unfortunately, most pastors today do not want to offend their members, so they preach nice little messages that don't offend anybody. There is little mention of a bloody cross on which a Savior died. Hence, our gospel has no power to save. But the early church preached a crucified Christ.

"But we preach Christ crucified, unto the Jews a stumblingblock, and unto the Greeks foolishness" (1 Corinthians 1:23).

But we fail today to preach *"Christ crucified"* because we do not want to offend anyone in a day of political correctness. Therefore, we refuse to address our hearers as sinners. We don't make mention of sin, we don't speak of man's duty of repentance, we don't warn of a future judgment for all mankind, we don't preach on the dangers of damnation in a Devil's hell. But we have a lot of comedians in the pulpit today with funny jokes and stories that will make you laugh and forget that you will die in your sins and enter a Christless eternity of misery and torment!

Jesus suffered and died and was buried and He rose again and ascended back into heaven where He now sits at the right hand of the Father and He earned that right by way of a BLOODY CROSS! But we don't preach up the Blood anymore. We don't want to offend anyone so we have extracted all the teeth out of the gospel so it won't bite anybody. We don't sing about the Blood anymore when we have so-called worship time in our churches. We have wiped up all the Blood of the Savior out of our religion today and preach a bloodless Cross. There is no need to mention the Blood because we fail to preach against sin today. And if you fail to preach against sin then there is no need to preach man's duty of repentance and no need to speak of a Savior who shed His Blood for sinful man. All we have to say is: "God loves you. Believe in Him and you will go to heaven!" it's an "only believe" gospel and it has sent multitudes to Hell!

Why in our churches today do we no longer sing hymns about the Blood of Christ: "There is Power in the Blood"; "Nothing but the Blood of Jesus"; "There is a Fountain Filled with Blood". The Gospel is about blood redemption. That Christ entered the market place of sin and purchased us by His death and blood. Instead, we sing songs which glorify man's happiness in God. Rather than songs that glorify God!

But you don't have much of a gospel if you remove the Blood from it. And you don't have any gospel at all without mention of a bloodstained Christ who died for sin. We read in Revelation about blood redemption, *"Unto him that loved us, and washed us from our sins in his own blood"* (Revelation 1:5). The recovery of the Gospel is a recovery of the preaching of the Cross.

CHAPTER SIX
THE LORDSHIP OF CHRIST

"Christianity means self must be dethroned, and another enthroned there—The Lord Jesus Christ."

E. A. Johnston

The missing doctrine in the church today is the Lordship of Christ. It is doubtful you will hear much today from our pulpits regarding the cross in the life of a believer, even though Jesus spoke often on the subject.

"Then Jesus said unto his disciples, If any man will come after me, let him deny himself, and take up his cross, and follow me. For whosoever will save his life shall lose it: and whosoever shall lose his life for my sake shall find it. For what is a man profited, if he shall gain the whole world, and lose his own soul? or what shall a man gain in exchange for his soul" (Matthew 16:24-26)?

The terms of discipleship were laid out clearly by Christ Jesus.

"If anyone comes to me, and hate not his father, and mother, and wife, and

children, and brethren, and sisters, yea, and his own life also, he cannot be my disciple. And whosoever doth not bear his cross, and come after me, cannot be my disciple" (Luke 14:26-27).

Few today when making a public profession of Christ consider the cost of discipleship. Does anyone speak of it from our pulpits today? But Jesus said we must consider the cost in following a crucified Savior.

"For which of you, intending to build a tower, sitteth not down first, and counteth the cost, whether he have sufficient to finish it? Lest haply after he hath laid the foundation, and is not able to finish it, all that behold it begin to mock him. Saying, This man began to build, and was not able to finish. Or what king, going to make war against another king, sitteth not down first, and consulteth whether he be able with ten thousand to meet him that cometh against him with twenty thousand? Or else, while the other is yet a great way off, he sendeth ambassadors and desireth conditions of peace. So likewise, whoever he be of you that forsaketh not all that he

hath cannot be my disciple" (Luke 14: 28-33).

But most pastors today want to grow their congregations numerically because they judge their success in ministry by the size of their congregation and campus. If we are not running three thousand on Sunday we are not living up to our potential. So we water down the gospel message to make it more palatable to sinful man, so we can get "our converts" and fill seats in the sanctuary. We omit the doctrine of the cross in the life of a believer, even though Jesus never did! We fail to tell men and women and boys and girls that if you want Christ as your Savior then He must be your Lord!

But the doctrine of the Lordship of Christ has fallen to the wayside in our modern churches today. We don't want to offend anyone with an offensive gospel message about dying to yourself and taking up your cross in a life lived under the Lordship and rule of Christ Jesus!

> *"What? know ye not that your body is the temple of the Holy Ghost which is in you, which ye have of God, and ye are not your own? For ye are bought with a price: therefore glorify God in your body, and in your spirit, which are God's"* (1 Corinthians 6:19-20).

We fail to mention that when you become a Christian your life is no longer your own. Your money is not your own; your time is not your own; your body is not your own—Christ must be a Complete Master!

Mordecai Ham, a great evangelist of the last century (Billy Graham was converted in one of Ham's meetings) always preached the doctrine of the Lordship of Christ in all his meetings. And when he preached he turned towns upside down for God and the Gospel! It was said of Mordecai Ham:

> "When Evangelist Ham preached, mockers were converted, families were restored, bars were closed, laws were changed, churches were filled to overflowing (one even advertised in the paper that no more new converts should attend as there was not room for them), hundreds were called to preach, and crooked politicians either repented or feared the consequences. When some resisted God's work, God withdrew His grace in answer to Ham's prayers and God's judgment fell."[2]

---

[2] Dr. Bruce Miller, President International Bible College in his Introduction to biography of Mordecai Ham. 2005.

When evangelist Ham came to town he would go about trying to get his audience focused on the truth of the Lordship of Jesus Christ. We see this from the following:

> "I preached the absolute Lordship of Jesus Christ. I allowed for no compromise, but hammered this one thought that Christ Jesus must have first place, first call, and first allegiance. I made that the keynote of all my meetings. My objective has always been to enter a town and change the thinking of the residents toward Christ, to direct their lives to center on Christ."[3]

If we are to have a recovery of the Gospel of the Cross in your day and mine friend, then we must recover the lost doctrine of the Lordship of Christ!

> *"That at the name of Jesus every knee should bow, of things in heaven, and things in earth, and things under the earth: And that every tongue should confess that Jesus Christ is Lord, to the glory of God the Father"* (Philippians 2:10-11).

---

[3] Edward E. Ham, "50 Years On The Battle Front With Christ, A Biography of Mordecai Ham". (Nashville: The Hermitage Press, 1950), p 119.

CHAPTER SEVEN
AUTHORITY IN THE PULPIT

"Jesus must have preeminence in our lives, for Him to be prominent in our life."

E. A. Johnston

I had to face the reality of God that I had been living a sham religion with no power or presence of Christ Jesus. I wanted a life of victory, I truly desired consistency in my walk with God, but it was just failure, failure, failure! I asked God to show me why. Why didn't I have a life like Caleb where it was said of him, *"because thou hast wholly followed the LORD my God"* (Joshua 14:9).

I knew men of God personally who had this power in the pulpit. Men like Dr. Adrian Rogers and Dr. Stephen Olford, men that when they preached there was an authority from on high that attended their preaching. I knew they were both holy men of God, consecrated to the Lord. Why was I struggling so? In desperation I sought the Lord for an answer and I felt led to go to the Book of Hebrews in chapter two, where my eyes fell on the following verse:

"Thou hast put all things in subjection under his feet. For in that he put all in subjection under him, he left nothing

that is not put under him. But now we see not yet all things put under him" (Hebrews 2:8).

I have a Hebrew/Greek study Bible and I noticed that the word, "subjection" occurred twice in this verse, therefore it must be pretty important! I looked up the word, "subjection" in the Greek and it is the word "hupotasso" and it means:

(1) submit self unto
(2) submit oneself to be subject to be obedient
(3) voluntary submission
(4) submit ourselves to God's control

Then, after I had this understanding, I was led to focus on the last sentence of Hebrews 2:8 which states: *"But now we see not yet all things put under him"*. It was as if God was showing me through His Word that although my heart's desire was to be pleasing to Him in a consistent walk with Him, something was still LEFT UNDONE. Me, myself, and I, were not in SUBJECTION to Jesus as Lord of "all" in my life. Jesus had to have the PREEMINENCE in my life if I was to know the reality of Christ being PROMINENT in my life. He had to have First Place. First Priority. IN ALL THINGS. *"But now we see not yet all things put under him"* (Hebrews 2:8). I understand that this verse means that one day future after the Final Judgment and the final dissolution of the earth and its elements that all things THEN will be finally put under Him. But God was using this verse to speak to me PERSONALLY, as it applied to my life and walk with Him. I finally got it!

And I remembered a story that Adrian Rogers shared one day at Bellevue Baptist Church where I was a member. He told the following story:

"I had the privilege to preach in Romania shortly after God brought spiritual revival to this nation that had been liberated from a cruel Communist government. One of the leaders in that revival was a man named Josef T'son. Part of what made this man a mighty servant of the Lord was his exercise of Kingdom Authority in his life. Suffering at the hands of the Communists with brutal beatings, imprisonments, and death threats, he learned the victory that comes so sweetly in surrendering to the Savior.

"As Josef and I rode along in his car, I said, "Josef, tell me about American Christianity."

"He said, "Adrian, I had rather not."

"I said, "No, I want to know."

"He then said, "Well, Adrian, since you have asked me, I'll tell you. The key word in American Christianity is 'commitment.'""

"I said, "That is good, isn't it, Josef?""

"He replied, "No, it is not. As a matter of fact, the word 'commitment' did not come into great usage in the English language until about the 1960's. In Romania we do not even have a word to translate the English word 'commitment'. If you were to use 'commitment' in your message tonight, I would not have a proper word to translate it with.""

"Josef continued, "When a new word comes into usage, it generally pushes an old word out. I began to study and found the old word that 'commitment' replaced, Adrian, the old word that is no longer in vogue in America is the word 'surrender'.""

"Josef," I asked. "What is the difference between 'commitment' and 'surrender'?"

"He said, "When you make a commitment you are still in control, no matter how noble the thing you commit to. One can commit to pray, to

study the Bible, to give his money, or to commit to automobile payments, or to lose weight. Whatever he chooses to do, he 'commits' to. But 'surrender' is different. If someone holds a gun and asks you to lift your hands in the air as a token of surrender, you don't tell that person what you are committed to. You simply surrender and do as you are told."

"He said, "Americans love commitment because they are still in control. But the key word is 'surrender'. We are to be the slaves of the Lord Jesus Christ."[4]

I finally understood why men like Adrian Rogers and Stephen Olford possessed such power in the pulpit, for when they preached they preached with Heaven's authority. It was because these men of God were in SUBJECTION to Christ as Lord in their lives over ALL THINGS. They were men full of the Holy Ghost and to get "that" one must serve Jesus as a Complete Master.

I challenge every preacher reading this book to get alone with God and get serious with God over this issue of authority in the pulpit. Can it be said of

---

[4] Dr. Adrian Rogers, sermon preached at Bellevue Baptist Church, Cordova, TN).

you friend, that *"But now we see not yet all things put under him"* (Hebrews 2:8). Are you holding back something from the Lord Jesus that He wants you to give to Him?

Christ gave His all on Calvary, holding nothing back! How can we hold anything back from Him? God gets serious with those who get serious with Him. God declares, *"Return unto me, and I will return unto you, saith the LORD of hosts"* (Malachi 3:7).

CHAPTER EIGHT

UNCTION: POWER IN THE PULPIT

> "If we serve such a dynamite God, then how come so many of us are living firecracker lives?"

> Vance Havner

I had an appointment with my homiletical mentor, Dr. Stephen F. Olford, and I was seated in his study awaiting his arrival. He came in and he looked exhausted. He sunk into his chair and said,

> "Pardon me brother, I must have some time to regather myself. I must regather myself, I have just finished preaching and virtue has left me."

Immediately, a text came to my mind from Matthew's Gospel where the woman with the issue of blood reaches out and touches the hem of Jesus's garment and she was instantly healed. And Jesus turned about and remarked, "Who touched me?" and His disciples in wonder say in so many words, "Master, look around you at this crowd pressing against you and you say, 'Who touched me?'" (Mark 5:21-34).

The word for virtue in the Greek is the word, "dunamis" (where we get our English word dynamite) which means power. Power had left

Jesus when the woman touched Him. And Dr. Olford was stating the same thing: when he preached, he preached with incarnational power from an anointing of the Spirit of God and virtue had left him! Let me ask you brother preacher: when you preach does virtue leave you?

The Apostle Paul told the church at Corinth:

"And my speech and my preaching was not with enticing words of man's wisdom, but in demonstration of the Spirit and of power" (1 Corinthians 2:4).

We who preach the Gospel should preach it *"in demonstration of the Spirit and of power."* (1Cor. 2:4) In fact, Dr. Martyn Lloyd-Jones said that we are not preaching if we are not preaching *"in demonstration of the Spirit and of power."* The Holy Spirit must attend the preaching of God's Word for transformation to occur in the lives of our hearers. But sadly, many stand impotent in our pulpits today, void of any power from on high.

Jesus gave specific instructions to His disciples before He ascended back into heaven:

"And said unto them, Thus it is written, and thus it behooved Christ to suffer and to rise from the dead the third day. And that repentance and remission of sins should be preached in his name

among all nations beginning at Jerusalem. And ye are witnesses of these things. And, behold, I send the promise of my Father upon you: but tarry ye in the city of Jerusalem until ye be endued with power from on high" (Luke 24:46-49).

We must ask ourselves this burning question: Do we know anything of this *"enduement from on high"*? Jesus instructed His men to *"tarry"* to "wait", wait in prayer until they received this special anointing of the Spirit of God. I submit to you friend, not much good will be done if we preach without this power. Not much good as far as things of eternal worth are concerned. It is the Holy Spirit who transforms lives under an anointed ministry. There is a close connection to preaching and prayer. E. M. Bounds speaks of this very thing in his book, *"Preacher and Prayer"*:

> "What of unction? It is the indefinable in preaching which makes it preaching. It is that which distinguishes and separates preaching from all mere human addresses. It is the divine in preaching. It makes the preaching sharp to those who need sharpness. It distills as the dew to those who need to be refreshed.

"This unction comes to the preacher not in the study but in the closet. It is heaven's distillation in answer to prayer. It is the sweetest exhalation of the Holy Spirit. It impregnates, suffuses, softens, percolates, cuts, and soothes. It carries the Word like dynamite, like salt, like sugar; makes the Word a soother, an arraigner, a revealer, a searcher; makes the hearer a culprit or a saint, makes him weep like a child and live like a giant; opens his heart and his purse as gently, yet as strongly as the spring opens the leaves. This unction is not the gift of genius. It is not found in the halls of learning. No eloquence can woo it. No industry can win it. No prelatical hands can confer it. It is the gift of God—the signet set to his own messengers. It is heaven's knighthood given to the chosen true and brave ones who have sought this anointed honor through many an hour of tearful, wrestling prayer.

"Earnestness is good and impressive; genius is gifted and great. Thought kindles and inspires, but it takes a diviner endowment, a more powerful energy than earnestness or genius or thought to break the chains of sin, to win estranged and depraved hearts to God, to repair the breaches and restore the Church to her old ways of purity and power. Nothing but this holy unction can do this."[5]

To which we speak of here, this unction, this power in the pulpit, is a lost art today in ministry for very few have it, let alone know what it is. It is something that can only be attained if sought with a sincere heart and with right motives for the good of the kingdom and the glory of God. No self-promotion, self-advancement or self-glory can attain this divine touch from on High. When self is in the way then God leaves us to our self. When one examines Christian biography of those whom God has used in mighty ways, there is often found a common denominator that links their illustrious careers for Christ and the Gospel. One is familiar with the names of Charles Grandison Finney, Dwight Lyman Moody, and Samuel Porter Jones. But few are aware of the fact that all three of these evangelists: Charles Finney, D. L. Moody, and Sam Jones had this unction from on High "before" they entered their larger public ministry. Some would

---

[5] E. M. Bounds, "Preacher and Prayer" and Marion Price, "Never Quit Praying for Your Loved Ones, two volumes in one with a Foreword by Dr. E. A. Johnston, (Asheville: Revival Literature, 2013). pp 68-70.

call this experience "A Second Blessing." Moody was fine with that terminology. If you want to preach with power then read carefully the following story of these three men who found this power.

> "It is no coincidence that the three most-used American evangelists of the 19th century each shared a common experience—an enduement of Holy Ghost power for service. It happened to Charles Finney, D. L. Moody, and Sam Jones. This was the secret to their power. And this anointing occurred to each of them BEFORE they were thrust onto a national stage of greater usefulness.

> "It came to Dwight Lyman Moody in 1871, before he was greatly used of God in revival throughout Great Britain. It happened to Charles Grandison Finney before he was used of God in revivals during the Second Great Awakening. And it happened to Samuel Porter Jones before he was used in revivals throughout the whole of America. We will examine these men one by one and compare their unique yet common experience.

> "In 1871 D. L. Moody was hungering for something more for God.

"An intense hunger and thirst for spiritual power was aroused in him by two women who used to sit in the front seat. He could see by the expression on their faces that they were praying. At the close of the service they would say to him:

"'We have been praying for you.'"

"'Why don't you pray for the people?' Mr. Moody would ask.

"'Because you need the power of the Spirit,' they would say.

"There came a great hunger in my soul. I did not know what it was. I began to cry out as I never did before. I really felt that I did not want to live if I could not have this power for service."

"D. L. Moody would speak of his experience of 1871 in future sermons and considered it the watermark highlight of his effectiveness for Christ and the gospel. Even near the end of his life in his last campaign he would make mention of it.

"I was crying all the time that God would fill me with His Spirit. Well, one day, in the city of New York---oh, what a day!---I cannot describe it. I seldom refer to it, it is almost too sacred an experience to name. Paul had an experience of which he never spoke for fourteen years. I can only say that God revealed Himself to me, and I had such an experience of His love that I had to ask Him to stay His hand. I went to preaching again. The sermons were no different; I did not present any new truths, and yet hundreds were converted. I would not now be placed back where I was before that blessed experience if you should give me all the world---it would be as the small dust of the balance."

"Charles Finney had an identical experience of that of D. L. Moody, as we see from his Memoirs; he was newly converted and alone in his law office when the following incident occurred in 1821:

"But as I returned and was about to take a seat by the fire, I received a mighty baptism of the Holy Ghost...the Holy Spirit descended upon me in a manner that seemed to go through me, body and soul. I could feel the impression, like a wave of electricity, going through and through me. Indeed it seemed to come in waves, and waves of liquid love;—for I could not express it in any other way…these waves came over me, and over me, and over me one after the other, until I recollect I cried out, 'I shall die if these waves continue to pass over me.' I said to the Lord, "Lord, I cannot bear anymore."'"

Samuel Porter Jones, before God used him in a larger capacity of national prominence and city-wide revivals, he received the same anointing of Holy Ghost power as did Finney and Moody. Connecting the three dots of these three evangelists in revival by a common denominator of spiritual experience has never before been made public or printed until now. They each shared 'the Secret'."

Sam Jones was holding meetings in Corinth, Mississippi, in 1884 (prior to his being thrust into national prominence), when the following incident occurred:

> "One of the most thrilling experiences of his life occurred there. He had become so wearied and tired from constant preaching that one night going to church he said, 'I am so tired I cannot stand up and preach this evening. I shall ask the people if they will allow me to sit down and talk to them.'

"Upon announcing his text, the baptism of the Holy Spirit came upon him, and when he had finished the sermon, and had concluded a long altar service, he went away from the church saying, 'I feel as if I were the best rested man on earth.' That night in his room, the Holy Spirit continued to bless him, until he cried out, 'This is glorious, the breezes of heaven are sweeping in upon my soul!' For ten minutes or more these waves of blessing passed over his spirit, and for three months or more he didn't know the sense of fatigue as he labored day and night for the salvation of the lost."[6]

This unction for power in the pulpit is from the anointing of the Spirit. My homiletical mentor, Dr. Stephen F. Olford wrote the key to this filling of the Spirit:

"The anointing of the Spirit: CONDITIONS

1) Holiness
2) Yieldedness
3) Prayerfulness"

---

[6] E. A. Johnston, "Sam Jones A New Biography", (Gainesville: The Old Paths Publications, 2023) pp 185-188.

CHAPTER NINE
THE LAST JUDGMENT

"The Holy Spirit moved mightily amongst us. The listeners felt as though they were at the judgment stand. A total of 1,363 repented and 80 people dedicated their lives to become preachers."

John Sung,
Singapore Revival,
1935.

I was preaching in the Southern part of the United States years ago and revival came. I had spent the evening out of bed and on my knees wondering what I was to preach that Sunday morning. I had no sermon prepared. I had only a burden upon my heart for lost sinners. That particular Sunday morning I preached on the striking passage of Scripture found in the Book of Revelation in chapter twenty which described the final judgment day of all mankind where the final dissolution of all things took place and men were judged according to their works as they faced a Judge on a great white throne.

"And I saw a great white throne, and him that sat on it, from whose face the earth and the heaven fled away, and

there was found no place for them. And I saw the dead, small and great, stand before God, and the books were opened: and another book was opened, which is the book of life: and the dead were judged out of those things which were written in the books, according to their works. And the sea gave up the dead which were in it; and death and hell delivered up the dead which were in them: and they were judged every man according to their works. And death and hell were cast into the lake of fire. This is the second death. And whosoever was not found written in the book of life was cast into the lake of fire" (Revelation 20: 11-15).

The Last Judgment is seldom preached anymore. But I preached that message that morning in that church and God took over the service. Halfway through my message it looked as if a cannon ball had been shot right down the center aisle of that church! There was a look of alarm on the faces of the people. We seemed to all be standing on the very verge of eternity looking into the final destiny of mankind before God! There was a bubbling burning lake spitting fire and a holy Great White Throne with God sitting there in Judgment on every mother's son! There was no escaping that terrible scene of a Final Judgment for all mankind.

And when it came time for me to give the invitation, I asked for the deacons to come down front to be available for counseling of any who had a desire to be saved—but no one moved. No one budged. I thought they didn't hear me or they didn't understand me so I repeated my request for the deacons to come down front for counseling—but it was completely still in that sanctuary. No one moved. I closed my Bible and left the platform taking a seat on the front row with my back to the congregation. I couldn't take it any longer I JUST WANTED TO WORSHIP A HOLY GOD! So I dropped to the floor in front of my seat and raised my arms over my head in celebration and worship of the Lamb who was slain for a poor sinner like me! Suddenly, there was motion behind me as a young man ran up the aisle of the church, hollering as loud as he could, "I just got saved! I just got saved! I really just got saved!" he was jumping up and down for joy. Others began to come forward. A deacon approached me and apologized to me, he said, "We could not respond to your request to come counsel we were frozen in our seats and could not move!" The music minister approached me with a big grin on his face exclaiming, "I saw Jesus sitting on His throne!" Revival came that day and God did a work amidst His people. Why? Did the visiting preacher tell funny stories from the platform to warm up his crowd? NO. I spoke to them with a broken heart and with a burden for their souls and with tears in my eyes I pleaded with them to face their eternity and the God of that eternity as I preached on the Final Judgment Day. And God showed up.

When will we stop all the nonsense? When will we stop telling jokes in the pulpit and trying to be comedians and entertainers to amuse people and make them laugh? When will we be honest with folks and warn them of the dangers of damnation in a Devil's Hell! Why don't we preach hard against sin? Why don't we warn men of their duty of repentance? Why don't we inform men of their utter necessity of regeneration by the Spirit of God in the conversion of a soul? Why, oh why, don't we warn folks of a final Judgment that awaits all mankind where every mother's son will be held up against the strictness and severity of God's unbending Law! Where books will be opened and cases reviewed under the intense scrutiny of a thrice holy Judge! Where men will be found guilty and sentence carried out for the sentencing of the law must be carried out upon all guilty lawbreakers! Why are we derelict in our duty to warn men? We ourselves are warned to warn others:

> *"Son of man, I have made thee a watchman unto the house of Israel: therefore hear the word at my mouth, and give them warning from me. When I say unto the wicked, Thou*

shalt surely die, and thou givest him not warning, nor speakest to warn the wicked from his wicked way, to save his life; the same wicked man shall die in his iniquity; but his blood will I require at thine hand. Yet if thou warn the wicked, and he turn not from his wickedness, nor from his wicked way, he shall die in his iniquity: but thou hast delivered thy soul" (Ezekiel 3:17-19).

I fear many preachers will be standing before God on That Day with BLOODY HANDS! Because they failed to preach the whole counsel of God and warn men to flee from the wrath to come! They didn't want to bruise their reputation. They wanted to be liked by their people so they gave them what they wanted, soothing messages, rather than giving them what they needed—the real Gospel of the Cross of the Son of God! This is why we desperately need a recovery of the true Gospel in our day. We need men who will be called of God to preach the Word of God fearlessly for God to a generation of the Hell bound! We need men like these:

"The Apostle Paul, Luther, Wesley, Whitefield, Knox, Edwards, Finney, Spurgeon, Moody, each shared a common denominator: a fire in their belly. They each were so eaten up with the Gospel and thirsty for Christ and filled with the Holy Ghost---they could not stand idly by while others perished. They saw nothing but eternity, worshipped a Holy God, and served a Risen Christ; living not for earth nor its gains but living only for heaven and its rewards. When they preached they linked the Devil with sin and the Cross with salvation. They preached hell and its fire and Christ and Him crucified. Not one of them feared King, Queen, or Pope; and not one of them sought the compliments of man."

E. A. Johnston

I hope this little book has been of some help to you friend. I have included some of my sample sermons to give you an idea of how this old preacher preaches the real undiluted Gospel of the Son of God! May God bless you as you serve Him in these Last Days—all for His glory!

CHAPTER TEN

SAMPLE SERMONS

"Our greatest need today is for God-called preachers to preach a God-centered Gospel of the Cross in the power of the Holy Ghost and invite poor lost sinners to come to a blood-stained Christ for pardon of sin. The hyper-Calvinism of our day would have left Zaccheus stuck up a tree."

E. A. Johnston

Gospel Sermon #1:

GOOD ENOUGH FOR HEAVEN AND NOT BAD ENOUGH FOR HELL

(This sermon was preached December 30th, 2024. Bible text: Romans 3:23).

Years ago, a friend of mine asked me to go visit his dying aunt who was in the hospital. At her bedside I introduced myself as her nephew's friend, and after some small talk, I asked her a question. I asked: "When it comes time for you to die, do you know for sure if you're going to heaven?" She answered, "Yes." I said, "Why are you so certain?" She informed me she had been a member in good standing in the Methodist Church for thirty years. I replied, "Some folks mistake church membership for salvation." She shook her head and told me she was going to heaven because she'd never robbed a liquor store or killed anyone. That's what the "old gal" said. She had made up her mind that she was going to heaven when she died because she was good enough for heaven and not bad enough for hell.

The majority of mankind thinks that way. That they are good enough for heaven because they are not bad enough for hell. They believe only really "bad" people go to hell, like murderers, serial killers, or sociopaths. Everybody else is a hard-working, honest person who helps their neighbors and they are "good" people. They are loving and they are loved by their loved ones and when they die they go straight to heaven. Just listen to how the world talks when someone dies. They'll say, "Well at least he's not suffering anymore." We comfort the grieving family members by saying, "I know you miss him but look at it this way—at least he's no longer in any pain." That's how people think, that at the end of the road when it comes time to die heaven is waiting, where there is no longer any suffering or any tears. You will hear, "My Daddy was a good man. Why he'd help anybody! He's up there with God now."

But the trouble is, "good people" don't go to heaven—only "forgiven people" get to go there!

Now, all babies who die will go to heaven—you don't have to worry about them. I have a baby in heaven myself. We get comfort from the Bible on this: *"And he said, While the child was yet alive, I fasted and wept: for I said, Who can tell whether God will be gracious to me, that the child may live? But now he is dead, wherefore should I fast? can I bring him back again? I shall go to him, but he shall not return to me"* (2 Samuel 12:22-23).

But heaven is barred against anyone who isn't born from above and washed in the Blood of Christ Jesus. If you die in your sins, you'll bust hell wide open when you die! God will not allow any rebel into His kingdom who is still pointing a shotgun of rebellion at Him. You see friends, most folks believe they are good enough for heaven because they are not bad enough for hell. But the truth is, from the Bible's standpoint, all men are rebels against God and they are in a perishing lost condition because they are under the condemnation of a thrice-holy God who must punish sin! The sentencing of the law must be carried out upon all guilty lawbreakers. Sin is transgression of the law, so says the Word of God (1 John 3:4) and the God of the Word says, "and will by no means clear the guilty" (Exodus 34:7).

So the reality is when it comes time to die, most folks enter a Christless eternity and are damned in a Devil's hell! God says, no one is good enough for heaven because all men are bad enough for hell. So most folks hope of heaven is only a hole in the wall.

That's my introduction to my message this evening, entitled, "Good Enough For Heaven And Not Bad Enough For Hell." Young person, you listen to this old preacher! Don't assume you're automatically going to heaven because you were raised in the church. Church membership is not salvation. A lot of folks assume that their religion is their free ticket to heaven or a place called Paradise. They wrap themselves in the robes of their religion by either being a good Muslim, a good Mormon, a good Jew, a good Buddist, or a good Baptist! If religion got folks into heaven then why did Jesus speak so vehemently against the Pharisees and the Scribes, calling the vipers and children of the Devil—Jesus pronounced "woes" upon them!

RELIGION WON'T SAVE YOU

Only repentance towards God and faith in Jesus Christ saves. There is no such thing as a Christian who has never repented. Most of the opposition I've encountered preaching in churches has been on the doctrine of repentance. I've had angry deacons face me with fire in their eyes, when I said you must repent or surely go to hell! God sees all men as guilty rebels with enmity in their hearts against Him—they crucified His Son! And God is angry with the wicked day and night, so says the Word of God in Psalm 7:11. Unsaved man in his natural state is Hellbound, no matter how good a person he is. Trying to work your way to heaven by a good opinion of yourself and a long track record of religious service is like trying to climb up to heaven on a rope of sand! It can't be done. The good Catholic or good Baptist is as Hellbound as any other lost religious person who isn't regenerate by the Spirit of God.

YOU MUST BE BORN AGAIN

You must be born from above and if you don't repent and die you will surely go to hell even if you are the Chairman of the deacons! In the Book of Job we read of the fate of the unsaved: "Hell is naked before him, and destruction hath no covering" (Job 26:6). If you are not under Christ's Blood then you're good enough for hell friend. We are born with a ruined nature and a bent toward sin. You must be born from above and washed in the Blood—you must get to Jesus. Jesus is the only remedy and refuge for sin! He is the Pearl of great price, worth selling all for so He can be gained. In John 14:6 Jesus says, "I am the way, the truth, and the life: no man cometh unto the Father but by me." Here Jesus answers the three greatest questions of the human heart:

"How can I be saved?"

Jesus says, "I am the way."

"How can I be sure?"

Jesus says, "I am the truth."

"How can I be satisfied?"

Jesus says, "I am the life."

He is the bread of life. In John 6:35 Jesus says: *"I am the bread of life: he that cometh to me shall never hunger; and he that believeth on me shall never thirst."* Salvation is saving faith in Christ Jesus. But I fear many in our churches today have only believed the fact that Jesus died for sin, without believing on the Christ who died! You must get to Christ and own Him as Savior and Lord.

Listen friend: Jesus came into this world doing good, healing the sick; feeding the hungry; giving sight to the blind; even raising the dead to life. Yet what happened? Men cried, Away with Him! and nailed Him to a Cross. Putting Him to death exposed the enmity of man's wicked heart against God. So they crucified Him. in Matthew's Gospel we read:

"Then the soldiers of the governor took Jesus into the common hall and gathered unto him the whole band of soldiers. And they stripped him, and put on him a scarlet robe. And when they had plaited a crown of thorns, they put it upon his head, and a reed in his right hand: and they bowed the knee before him, and mocked him, saying, Hail, King of the Jews! And they spit upon him, and took the reed and smote him on the head. And after that they had mocked him they took the robe off from him and put his own raiment on him, and led him away to crucify him."

And as those Roman soldiers took those nails and fastened the Son of God to that tree, every stroke of the hammer was an exclamation point, crying out: GOD MUST PUNISH SIN! GOD MUST PUNISH SIN! GOD MUST PUNISH SIN!

Look at that Man on the Cross friend! Look at that blessed Man on the Cross! See Him there, with His arms outstretched, beckoning you to come to him and believe on Him! Look at that bloodstained Savior for sin! He cries: *"Look unto me, and be ye saved all the ends of the earth; for I am God and there is none else"* (Isaiah 45:22).

Look at that Lamb on that bloody Cross friend! He is bearing the terrible weight of sin! My rotten sins! Your filthy sins! See Him as He pleads: *"Come now, and let us reason together, saith the LORD: though your sins be as scarlet, they shall be as white as snow; though they be red like crimson, they shall be as wool"* (Isaiah 1:18).

The Cross is the place where men sought to get rid of Him, but by His death it becomes the place where His saving power flows out to all who come in repentance, confessing they are sinners, and own Him as Savior and Lord! If you've not trusted this

Blessed Savior, receive Him now before it's too late! Soon He will come in judgment on this world, when His anger shall burn as an oven, (Malachi 4:1), and then you shall meet Him as your Judge!

COME NOW! COME TO JESUS! COME! YOUNG LADY DON'T WAIT ANY LONGER! WHAT ARE YOU WAITING FOR MISTER? DON'T WAIT UNTIL YOU'RE BETTER! COME TO JESUS! BRING TO HIM YOUR HEARTACHE! BRING TO HIM YOUR FEARS! BRING TO HIM YOUR SIN BURDEN AND LEAVE IT AT HIS NAIL-PIERCED FEET!

Listen to the last gospel invitation in the Bible, it may be for you your last invitation to come. Even if you're the biggest sinner in this town tonight—there's room at the Cross for you! There is a fountain filled with Blood, drawn from Immanuel's veins, and sinners plunged beneath that flood, lose all their guilty stains! Don't' delay friend. If you hear God's Voice speaking to your heart tonight, you come, come to the only remedy for sin in the Person of Christ Jesus. Listen to this final gospel plea:

> *"And the Spirit and the bride say, Come. And let him that heareth say, Come. And let him that is athirst come. And whosoever will, let him take the water of life freely!"* (Rev. 22:17)

LIKE MUSTARD ON A BLUE SUIT

(This sermon was preached on Sunday, November, 10, 2024. Bible text: Revelation 20:11-15).

Let me pray:

"Great and terrible God in heaven, you are high and lifted up, whose name is holy. You dwell among the cherubim. Help me, I pray, Lord, to deliver this message that you have burning in my soul. I pray, great God, though Satan roar and hellish hosts revile forever, let me preach this message in the demonstration of the Spirit and of the power of God.

Bring a soul out of the kingdom of darkness into the kingdom of light and life. Open hearts, I pray, and reveal your Son as the pearl of great price who's worth selling all for and losing all for so he may be gained. For what profits a man if he gains the world, but loses his soul? There are some here tonight, Lord, who may be in danger of losing their soul. The devil's got four aces on them, their heart is as hard as a rock, but you say, Lord, in your word, that your word is a hammer that breaks the rock in pieces. And Lord, I ask you tonight to come and bust things up here! Bust up every false foundation of an empty religious profession. Bust up every false hope. Break apart every false refuge of carnal security. And Lord, there are people here sound asleep in their sins. You say that your word is like a fire, come burn someone's conscience in this message and awaken them to their lost condition and alarm them to their perilous position of dying in their sins and experiencing the terrible consequences of damnation in a devil's hell!

Great God, you also declare that your word is like a two-edged sword that divides asunder. I pray, great God, that by your Spirit you come here tonight and cut somebody up to pieces! Hew them down like Samuel hacked up old rotten King Agag. Open hearts tonight, I pray. Pull the curtains down on eternity. Let sinners tremble as they totter over the bottomless pit and dangle there like a worm being fed to a raven! Wake up these lost religious people, Lord, I pray. Save some of them before you remove them and send them to hell! You are a God who must punish sin. As those soldiers nailed up your Son, Jesus, to that cross, every stroke of the hammer was an exclamation point crying out, GOD MUST PUNISH SIN! GOD MUST PUNISH SIN! GOD MUST PUNISH SIN! Lord, I pray that your Spirit come among us and disturb folks. Let those here get a glimpse of heaven, hell, and eternity! I pray these things in the strong name of Jesus. Amen."

Well, let me gather myself a minute, friends. I plumb wore myself out here before I even got started. I've got a serious message for us this evening, friends, and it's a solemn warning, like the words of the prophet Jeremiah, "But his word was in my heart as a burning fire shut up in my bones." This message is burning in my bones, and I'm coming to you tonight friends, like a smoking volcano erupting with warning! The hour is late and Christ's return is near. Like the Apostle says, "It is high time to awake out of sleep. The night is far spent. The day is at hand. Let us therefore cast off the works of darkness and put on the armor of light."

Do you believe, friends, that we're living in the last days? Do you believe we're living in dark days? Does it appear to you that the devil has the highway and society is in moral chaos and spinning out of control? Then why do you halt between two opinions, friend? If the Lord be God, follow Him, but if Baal, then follow him. Baal was an idol that was just the face of the devil. The idol you serve friend, is really the devil. You can't play footsie with God in partial obedience. You're either 100 percent sold out to Him or you're not. You can't have it both ways. You can't have one foot with God and one foot in the world. It's either God or Baal. You better settle this tonight friend, or it'll be hell to pay.

I'm going to preach the unvarnished Gospel to you tonight, friends, and like we say in the South, I'm gonna give you the oil straight from the can. So sit up straight and get the wax out of your ears. God will do business tonight with those who want to do business with Him.

I was playing golf with a giant of a man. He stood six foot five and was as wide as a brick wall, and every time this big man took a swing at the ball he cursed God and cussed man. He had the filthiest mouth of any man I ever heard. I couldn't take it anymore, so finally I turned to him on a tee box and said "Can I ask you a question?" He said, "Shoot." I said, "How is your relationship with God?" He smiled a big grin and said, "Fine. I have a great relationship with God. I leave Him alone and He leaves me alone!" That's what the big man said. Do you know what friend? It breaks my heart to say it, all you have to do to go to hell is for God to leave you alone. If you're here tonight and you are saved, it's because God gave you saving faith. Salvation is in the hands of God.

Well, that's my little introduction, friends. Let's get down to business. We've got a lot of ground to cover tonight. Let me share a story with you first. Years ago, I was preaching in a church down South in Mississippi, one Sunday morning, and it was customary down South after the service to have a big smorgasbord for the visiting preacher. Well, we all went to the fellowship hall where picnic tables were ready. At a long table buffet food was lined up there. Well, I like hot dogs, so I loaded up my plate with a few hot dogs, and I like mustard on my hot dogs; some of you kids might like mustard on your hot dogs as well. So I lathered them up from a jar of mustard on the table that was before me. I sat down with an old deacon and his wife, and I wondered why they were staring at me so, until I realized I had smeared yellow mustard all over the front of my brand new blue suit. The old deacon shook his head and said, "Well, at least we know you're human."

I took that suit to the cleaners, but that mustard stain never came out of that blue suit. It always had a green hue. Every time after that, when I wore that suit and looked in the mirror, it always carried that stain and that's what sin does to you, friend. It stains you, and it won't come out. it won't come off of you. You can try to whitewash sin by calling it other names, but that won't do. A fib is still a lie. Taking something that doesn't belong to you is still stealing. Fooling around is still adultery. You can't whitewash sin by renaming it. Now listen to me, friends: sin is still sin, and it leaves a stain on you morally that you can't wash out, even by church membership. My new blue suit had that mustard stain, and it's still there, even though the suit is old.

The title of my message this evening, friends, is, "Like Mustard On A Blue Suit," and my text can be found in the Book of Revelation. You can turn in your Bibles there now, friends, we will be in chapter 20. I drink coffee when I have my quiet time with the Lord, and I keep my Bible in my lap and I'm careful as to not spill any coffee, but one time I spilled coffee accidentally on a page of my Bible. Well, that brown stain never came out. Sin is like that in a book. God keeps a book on every one of us. In one day future, He will open the books and review our life, both the good and the bad. We see this to be the case in our text this evening from Revelation in chapter 20, beginning in verse 11.

> *"And I saw a great white throne, and him that sat on it, from whose face the earth and the heaven fled away; and there was found no place for them"* (Revelation 20:11).

Let me pause here friends, to say this speaks of the final judgment of all mankind and the final dissolution of the whole frame of nature. That great white throne speaks of a tribulation of judgment. It's a heavenly courtroom scene. The white of that throne symbolizes purity and holiness of a thrice-holy God. The judge of that throne is the judge of all the earth, and shall not the judge of all the earth do right? Well, let's take a look at who is appearing before that throne. Let's continue with our striking passage of Scripture.

> *"And I saw the dead, small and great, stand before God; and the books were opened: and another book was opened, which is the book of life: and the dead were judged out of those things which were written in the books, according to their works"* (Revelation 20:12).

Let me pause here again, friends, to say, well, what books are these being referenced to? There's a book of remembrance that contains both good and bad. It's the detailed biography of our life. God will open the books on us. The next book is the book of God's law and each man will be held up against the strictness and severity of God's unbending law and all will fail that test for all have sinned and come short of the glory of God. Those guilty lawbreakers will face the intense scrutiny of that judge.

Then, there is a book that decides one's eternal destiny, the book of life. Well, this heavenly courtroom scene where cases will be reviewed and evidence presented and examined, every word, every thought, every deed will be reviewed by the One who has eyes of fire!

Well, let's continue with our text, friends.

"And the sea gave up the dead which were in it: and death and hell delivered up the dead which were in them: and they were judged every man according to their works. And death and hell were cast into the lake of fire. This is the second death. And whosoever was not found written in the book of life was cast into the lake of fire" (Revelation 20:13-15).

I will stop there. Oh, what a solemn scene! It's a courtroom scene and, if I may so speak, where the Son of God is the judge, the angels are the bailiffs, and Satan is the prosecuting attorney—the accuser of the brethren. All of mankind stands there from every generation since Adam. Who will be justified and acquitted by that judge? Only those whose names are found written in the Book of Life.

There stands before that judge a vast crowd of people. There stands the antediluvians of Noah's day who rejected the preaching of Noah and who drowned in the flood. There stands the men of Sodom, who mocked righteous Lot, and who whom God rained fire and hell out of heaven and consumed them. There stands the Jewish religious leaders who shouted, "Crucify him!" There stands Pontius Pilate, who now himself is being judged by the one he judged. There stands the Caesars. There stands the kings and queens. There stands the potentates of every nation. There stands the presidents and leaders of every nation, from every continent, in every generation. There stands the rich and the poor, the famous and the unknown, the movers and the shakers, the small and the great. There stands your co-workers. There stands your neighbors. There stands your friends and family members. They face that righteous judge with the heat of that lake of fire burning behind them as it spits and spews and sizzles and torments those who are bound hand and foot and cast in there for all eternity!

How about you friend? How about you? How will you stand? Will you stand there with mustard on your blue suit? With the stain of sin on you? Will it be too late for change then, friend? I believe it'll be too late then, for as a tree falls, so it shall lay.

> *"He that is unjust, let him be unjust still: and he which is filthy, let him be filthy still: and he that is righteous, let him be righteous still: and he that his holy, let him be holy still"* (Revelation 22:11).

Like mustard on a blue suit, your sins will find you out. You'll be too late then, friend, and like mustard on a blue suit, you'll be found guilty of the stain of sin and breaking God's law and the sentencing of the law will be carried out by that judge who sits behind that pure great white throne as he announces the sentence against you.

> *"Then said the king to the servants. Bind him hand and foot, and take him away, and cast him into the outer darkness; there shall be weeping and gnashing of teeth"* (Matthew 22:13).

The suffering of the damned in hell is spoken of here. Weeping speaks of great loss and grief. Gnashing of teeth signifies great anger and regret. I speak to you tonight, friend, about the dangers of damnation in a devil's hell. Let me read you the verse that precedes the striking passage of Scripture about this great white throne judgment. In Revelation 20:10, we read:

> *"And the devil that deceived them was cast into the lake of fire and brimstone, where the beast and the false prophet are, and shall be tormented day and night for ever and ever"* (Revelation 20:10).

Do you want to be that destiny friend? Do you want that to be you? Will you admit that you're in danger? Will you admit that you're a guilty sinner? Will you admit that you've been hiding in the church for years under a profession of faith? Will you admit your hope of heaven is as empty as a hole in the wall? Will you turn to Christ now and repent of your sins? You're not in hell yet, friend. There is still time. There's still time to repent and surrender to God. Listen to God now as he declares.

"Come now, and let us reason together, saith the LORD: though your sins be as scarlet, they shall as white as snow; though they be red like crimson, they shall be as wool" (Isaiah 1:18).

Like mustard on a blue suit, sin stains the soul. Only the blood of Christ can wash away the stain of sin. You must be born from above and washed in the blood, friend. If you've not trusted this blessed Savior, receive Him now before it's too late! Soon He will come in judgement on this world when his anger shall burn as an oven and then you shall meet Him as your judge. Turn to God, friend, before it's too late. Surrender your all to Him. Jesus gave His all on Calvary, holding nothing back. How can you hold anything back from Him?

Come to Jesus. Come. What are you waiting for, mister? Don't wait until you're better. Come. Come to Jesus. The Gospel is for the weary, the hungry, and the thirsty. You must feel your need of a Savior for sin. Listen to this final Gospel call.

"And the Spirit and the bride say, Come. And let him that heareth say, Come. And let him that is athirst come.

And whosoever will, let him take the water of life freely" (Revelation 22:17).

Listen friends, the very last words of Jesus recorded in the Book of Revelation are these:

"Surely I come quickly" (Revelation 22:20).

WITHOUT JESUS YOUR SINS WON'T SINK

(This sermon was preached Tuesday, February 11, 2014. Bible text, Micah 7:19).

My message today friends is on how to get saved. I'd like to share with you a story about a rugged sea Captain who found Christ. It's a compelling story because Jesus came to save sinners, and sailors are often thought of as some of the rougher sort of men. The expression, "square like a sailor" pretty much sums up the seafaring life. A life on the sea is hard and it is a struggle to survive out on the wide ocean and the kind of men who end up being sailors are tough men and rough men and this particular sea Captain, that this story is about, was the roughest kind of sailor for he was a smuggler. He was not only a rough man but a lawless man. But God found him and he found God and he got saved and I want to tell you his story.

Before we begin, friends, I must give you some background on what it means to become a Christian, because in your day and mine, there is a famine for hearing the Word of God (Amos 8:11), and there are few preachers today who proclaim the true Gospel, the Gospel that has power to save. So I must share with you the Gospel before we proceed into the story of that smuggling sea Captain.

The title of my message today is, "Without Jesus Your Sins Won't Sink" and my text today is found in the Book of Micah, in chapter 7 and verse 19 which states,

> *"He will turn again, he will have compassion upon us; he will subdue our iniquities; and thou will cast all their sins into the depths of the sea"* (Micah 7:19).

When you hear the story of the sea Captain, you will know why I chose that text for us today. I will ask you to be patient with this poor preacher as I proceed because I must be honest with you and give you the Gospel with all its terrors and warnings and wooings. Like we say in the South, "I'm gonna give you the oil straight from the can." That means, I will not dilute the Gospel of the Son of God to make it more palatable for you to swallow, because your blood would be on my hands if I did that (Ezekiel 3:18). You see friends, we live in a day of a more modern gospel, a more politically-correct gospel, and one that has had all the teeth taken out of it. So, sit back and listen to the real thing before we get to our story today of the rugged sea Captain who got saved. I can assure you, friend, that without Jesus your sins won't sink!

I live in what's called "The Bible Belt" where there is a church on every corner but the problem is, the towns in which those churches exist grow more wicked with each new day. It makes me often wonder if there would be any noticeable impact on the town if the churches in those cities were replaced with libraries and coffee shops. Would it make any difference? The church is supposed to have an influence upon society but few do today because they have diluted the Gospel message to make it more palatable to sinful man. A preacher is supposed to be an ambassador for Christ (2 Corinthians 5:20) and represent Him and inform you of your duty of repentance and issue warning to flee from a terrible place called hell. That hell exists because of sin and for a person to avoid hell, and its fires, that person must be born again.

You see, friends, we've gotten mixed up on what the Gospel is and what the Gospel does. We have confused reformation and repentance. Reformation is cleaning ourselves up a little to be more presentable to man, but repentance is turning from our sins and turning to God. My fear is that because there is a shortage of hearing the true Gospel, there may be quite a large number of people who have never heard it, and what they call Christianity is just reformation. They decided to join the church, so they made some resolutions, they cleaned themselves up a little bit to fit in better among church people but the sad fact is, they probably never heard the Gospel come with power into their lives whereby they were transformed into a new creature and born again. They joined the church but they were never awakened to their lost condition and never convicted of sin by the Holy Spirit and they have never truly exercised repentance toward God and faith in Jesus Christ.

It may be, friend, you have never heard the true Gospel of the Son of God which speaks of a scandalous Cross on which the Prince of Glory died. That Cross had Christ's blood all over it! It was a bloody Cross because of sin. Sin is rebellion against God. God made man and placed him in a Garden and he blessed him with a good-looking wife, called Eve, and God gave man specific instructions not to eat of a certain tree in the Garden. But there was a serpent there, the devil, and he tempted Adam and Eve to rebel against God and commit sin. But when they sinned, they committed treason against the Almighty and He had no choice but to banish them from the Garden of Eden and banish them from His presence. Man fell that day into sin, and because of Adam's sin, all mankind enters this world with a sin nature, a depraved nature that is bent toward sin. Man drinks iniquity like its water (Job 15:16), and can't get enough of it, and man's dilemma is he can't get to God on his own. He is separated from God because of sin. His good works won't save him. His self-righteousness won't save him.

Man needs a sin substitute to get back to God. But why does man need a sin substitute? I'll tell you why: God requires perfection to get into His holy heaven. The benchmark God uses to test perfection is His holy law; His commands: do not lie, do not steal, do not commit adultery, do not covet, and so on. But the trouble is, man is a sinner and he has broken the law of God. God's law is strict and severe and when man is held up against the strictness and severity of God's unbending law, he will fail that test because man is a sinner and *"all have sinned and come short of the glory of God"* (Romans 3:23).

Listen friend, you're not a sinner because you sin, you sin because you are a big sinner! If you'd been in the Garden of Eden, you would have pushed Adam out of the way and tried to pull God down off His throne and sit there yourself! All sin is rebellion against God and sin separated man from God and there is no getting back to God on man's own merits. The Bible says our righteousness is as filthy rags in the sight of God (Isaiah 64:6).

Listen dear friend, all of mankind will face a future judgment. Hebrews 9:27 declares, *"And it is appointed unto men once to die but after this the judgment"* (Hebrews 9:27). Romans 14:10 states, *"We shall all stand before the judgment seat of Christ"* (Romans 14:10). The reason why man needs a sin substitute to get back to God, to be reconciled back to God, is because man cannot stand on his own merits and be held up against the strict and severe law of God and pass that test. Man is a law breaker, a guilty rebel against a Sovereign, who deserves punishment for sin, and the sentencing of the law must be carried out because God is a just judge who must punish sin! Just get out your Bible and read in Genesis how God sent a flood into the world in the days of Noah because of the wickedness of man, and God destroyed all of mankind except Noah and his family. Sin caused that flood, friend. Mankind was drowning in sin and God drowned them with a flood because God is a God who must punish sin.

Look again in Genesis, and see how God rained fire down upon wicked Sodom with an overthrow---reducing them to burnt ashes and black billowing smoke! Why? God is a God who must punish sin. The God of the Bible changes not (Malachi 3:6). He is still a God who hates sin and who will punish sin—so we need a sin substitute to get back to God. I know I am a sinner and I need a substitute for sin in the Person of Christ Jesus! And so do you friend, so do you!

Have you ever learned a foreign language? I took Spanish in High School but I was never good at it. Do you know what the language of the Gospel is?

I will tell you friend. The language of the Gospel is this: *"Except ye repent, ye shall all likewise perish"* (Luke 13:3). That's it in a nutshell from the lips of Christ Jesus. One must exercise repentance toward God and faith in Jesus Christ to enter heaven and be reconciled back to God. God will never save you while you are still pointing your shotgun of rebellion at Him! The only way to Jesus is to repent toward God. That means to throw down your shotgun of rebellion at the nail-pierced feet of a Sovereign. That means to submit to the claims and demands of the Lord Jesus Christ when you come to Him for salvation. Repentance is laying every inch of you on the altar of sacrifice and not holding anything back.

To get back to God, there must be a clean break with sin. But you won't hear much preaching on man's duty of repentance in your day and mine because most preachers have gotten out their mop buckets and mopped up all the blood and gore around Calvary, so it won't be offensive to anyone— let alone one hardened in sin. The message of the Cross isn't preached much anymore in day of sad spiritual declension in the church. But its only the blood of Christ that washes away sin, God's Word in Revelation declares, *"Unto him that loved us, and washed us from our sins in his own blood"* (Revelation 1:5). There is a cross in Christianity friends, and that Cross had Christ's blood all over it! The only way to get back to God is to get under that blood. Are your sins washed in the blood? The old hymn says: "What can wash away my sin, nothing but the blood of Jesus." And Cowper's hymn states, "There is a fountain filled with blood, drawn from Immanuel's veins and sinners plunged beneath that flood, lose all their guilty stains."

Let me ask you friend: Are you stained by sin? Our text today is from the Book of Micah and I will re-read it to you now:

> *"He will turn again, he will have compassion upon us; he will subdue our iniquities; and thou will cast all their sins into the depths of the sea"* (Micah 7:19).

Listen friend, when we come to Christ savingly, all of our sins are cast to the bottom of the sea never to rise again and indict us. But if you die in your sins, your sins won't sink, but they will line up one-by-one at the judgment bar, when your life is reviewed before God and you will be found guilty and the sentencing of the law will be carried out and you will be cast into a burning hell for all eternity! Hell is a place of torment where the worm dieth not and the damned cry out in agony and anguish. Jesus said hell is a region of weeping and gnashing of teeth. Weeping speaks of great loss and grief, gnashing of teeth signifies great anger and regret.

Listen friend, without Jesus your sins won't sink. Did you hear me? Without Jesus your sins won't sink! The Gospel declares: *"In whom we have redemption through his blood the forgiveness of sin according to the riches of his grace"* (Ephesians 1:7).

When I began this message, I promised you a story about a sea Captain and I intend to tell you that story right now, for this story of the smuggling sea Captain is a clear presentation of how to get back to God through the forgiveness of sin. Please, friend, listen carefully to the old sailor's story it's one of the best ones you'll ever hear! You may be able to relate to his predicament, you may find yourself in his shoes. This story may be a wonderful help to you! I have seldom heard a story so intriguing and so full of the Gospel of the Son of God as this one you are about to hear. His words speak life and death. Here now is his story:

"I was once the Captain of a smuggling boat. I remember well one morning, just at daybreak, we discovered a Coast Guard boat in the distance. We had on board a heavy cargo of tobacco and we stood to make quite a bit of money if we could land it. The Coast Guard was still a long way off but we knew that if she gave chase, we couldn't possibly get away because our heavy cargo slowed us so much. We hoped that first we might not be seen but alas, we soon saw the Coast Guard crowding all sail and turning her course toward us. We all knew what would happen if we were taken. Not only would the boat and cargo be confiscated, but we'd all be sent to prison.

"For a time, there was a dead silence while we stared at each other in dismay. The Coast Guard was coming up fast behind us. Suddenly, I thought of a way out. 'Mates!' I cried, 'there is no hope for us by running away but let them come. They will only find an empty ship.' Hastily, we first rigged the sail at the stern of the ship to screen us from the sight of the Custom's men. Then, sending part of the men below, I set them in line to hand up the packages of tobacco and pitched them overboard as they came up. Oh, how did we work!

"All was quiet. Nothing was heard but the splash of the tobacco dropping into the sea. The cargo was going down fast. 'Cheer up men!' I cried, 'we'll soon be finished with it.'

"Just then, I saw the ship's boy was too tired to go on so I sent him to see if the Coast Guard was very far off. In a minute, he came rushing back to me, pale as death. He just gasped out, 'It won't sink,' and then fled below.

"In a flash, we understood what he meant. I ran to the stern of the ship and what a sight that was. The sun was just rising behind us and there in that long line of light were the packages of tobacco bobbing up and down in our wake and the first package in line reached right back to the oncoming Coast Guard boat. Helplessly, we stood and stared at it. The proof of our guilt was there spread out for all to see. We were lost and in our ears rang over and over those fatal words, 'It won't sink.'

"In those days, my heart was far from God. I belonged to the world. From time-to-time though, I had serious thoughts and then I would resolve to correct my ways and change my course but resolving is one thing, doing is another. I still went on in the same old ways and as soon as we were free, I went back to smuggling.

"About three years after all this happened, I went out in a boat on the river one night. It was New Year's Eve and I spite of myself, my thoughts went back in review of my past life. I saw myself when a child, kneeling at my mother's knee to say my evening prayers. Again, I heard her tell me of One who come down from heaven to bring life to the world and at this I sighed deeply. The more I thought about my past, the more horrified I was. God had created me and I had lived and was still living as though there was neither God nor eternity.

"That night, I went down on my knees in the boat and prayed that God would come to my help. After this, I would be another man. I resolved not to touch a drop of liquor and to avoid all bad company. I made many more resolutions like that: what I would do and what I wouldn't do. Soon I began to feel a very good opinion of myself. Then, on further reflection, I saw that there were a lot more things I ought to clean up or lighten the ship as we say. I must throw overboard everything that ought not to be in my boat. My life was to be completely changed. My resolutions were getting more serious and positive every moment. My heart grew lighter and I was happy in the thought that I had become a new man.

"As a finishing stroke, I decided to sell my ship and go home to my mother. Having made the decision, it seemed as if everything must be in perfect order. I had taken up the oars to go back to land when suddenly the moon broke through the clouds and cast its beams like a band of silver across the water to where my boat was lying. But why should I start to shiver? What should it remind me of? The memory of that certain morning when chased by the Coast Guard I had cast a cargo into the sea came over me with overwhelming power. I saw again the ship's boy's frightened face and heard his cry, 'It won't sink!' How blind I was. Here again, I had tried to lighten my ship by casting the cargo overboard and there behold, it was all floating behind me like an accusing line stretched up to the throne of God. All that I had done, said or thought was there before the face of God and it would not sink. Fool that I was, I thought I could drown all my wickedness in the sea of eternal forgetfulness without a thought of the holiness of God. If I had been able from that moment on to do only what was good, it would not have changed the evil done in the past. What good was it to be forming good resolutions for the future and to pitch the old cargo overboard when it would not sink? Tears of despair filled my eyes I was hopelessly lost!

"While in this state, seeing neither relief nor safety, I remembered the teachings of my faithful mother. Had she often told me about Jesus, the Savior of sinners? Hadn't he died on the cross for sinners? And if I should turn to him now, wouldn't his precious blood wash away even my sins? Wasn't there grace and mercy even for me?

"All at once, everything was clear before me. Yes, the Lord Jesus had died for me. He had become the punishment of all my sins. If I accepted that, they would all be cast into the depths of the sea. 'Their sins and iniquities will I remember no more,' was the passage that kept coming to my mind. Such a joy filled my heart then. Lighthearted, entirely relieved of my burden, I turned my boat toward the shore and a new man, I stepped out onto the land. I had gone out a lost sinner but I was coming back redeemed by the Lord."

Like that sea Captain friend, you must come to Christ for forgiveness of sin. Without Jesus your sins won't sink! Jesus Christ is the only remedy for sin. Why wait any longer friend? Surrender your all to God and own Christ as Savior and Lord.

"He will turn again, he will have compassion upon us; he will subdue our iniquities; and thou will cast all their sins into the depths of the sea" (Micah 7:19).

FOUR PHOTOS

Author at D.L. Moody's Gravestone at
Round Top, Northfield, MA

Author at David Brainerd's Grave Marker at Bridge Street Cemetery, Northhampton, MA

Author at Asahel Nettleton Grave Marker at East Windser, CT

Author at the spot of George Whitefield's Last Open-Air Sermon Where He Preached to 4,000, Exeter, NH and Died the Next Morning

ABOUT THE AUTHOR

E.A. Johnston in the Outdoor pulpit at Hanham Mount where George Whitefield preached, courtesy of Digby James.

E. A. Johnston, Ph.D., D. B. S., is a Fellow with the Stephen Olford Institute for Biblical Preaching and is an evangelist and author with eighteen published books. He is the founder of Evangelism Awakening, a revival-based ministry whose focus is the study of historical revival and preaching for revival in our day. He has over two thousand sermons on SermonAudio.com.

SOME OF THE BOOKS BY E. A. JOHNSTON

Many of the following books may be purchased individually or as a set by going to Dr. Johnston's webpage in the bookstore at The Old Paths Publications that has links to distributors. Go to:

www.theoldpathspublications.com/Pages/Auth ors/Johnston.htm

or

Email us: TOP@theoldpathspublications.com

1. "A Heart Awake: The Authorized Biography of J. Sidlow Baxter" Foreword by Adrian Rogers (The Old Paths Publications, www.theoldpathspublications.com).
2. "Realities Of Revival" Foreword by Stephen F. Olford (Gospel Folio Press, Canada; 2005).
3. "No Turning Back" (Gospel Folio Press, Canada; 2005).
4. "The Master's Plan: Unfolding God's Blueprint For Your Life" (Gospel Folio Press, Canada; 2006).
5. "Know The Book: Bible Survey At A Glance" (Gospel Folio Press, Canada; 2007).

6. "Jua Kitabu: Tazamo la Biblia" Know The Book translated into the Swahili by missionary G. I. Harlow (Everyday Publications, Canada; 2007).

7. "Walking With God" Foreword by Ted S. Rendall (Gospel Folio Press, Canada; 2007).

8. "Return To Me: Entering A Right Relationship With God" (Gospel Folio Press, Canada; 2007).

9. "Are You In The Book Of Life?" (Gospel Folio Press, Canada; 2008).

10. "Call To Revival" Foreword By Colin Peckham (Gospel Folio Press, Canada; 2008).

11. "The Church In Revival" Foreword By Richard Owen Roberts (Gospel Folio Press, Canada; 2008).

12. "Olford On Scroggie: Stephen Olford's Notes on the Sermon Outlines of Graham Scroggie" Co-authored with Stephen Olford (The Old Paths Publications: www.theoldpathspublications.com).

13. "George Whitefield A Definitive Biography, Volumes 1 and 2 Combined" (The Old Paths Publications: www.theoldpathspublications.com).

14. "George Whitefield A Definitive Biography In Two Volumes" (American edition published by Revival Literature, Asheville; 2012).

15. "God's Hitchhike Evangelist The Biography Of Rolfe Barnard" Foreword By Bob

Doom (The Old Paths Publications: www.theoldpathspublications.com).

16. "Asahel Nettleton Revival Preacher" Foreword By John Thornbury, Preface By Richard Owen Roberts (The Old Paths Publications: www.theoldpathspublications.com).

17. "Sermons For Revival" (The Old Paths Publications: www.theoldpathspublications.com).

18. "A Noble Company Biographical Essays on Notable Particular Baptists in America Volume 11: Portrait of Rolfe Barnard" (Particular Baptist Press, Springfield; 2018).

19. "Lectures On Revival For A Laodicean Church," (The Old Paths Publications, www.theoldpathspublications.com)

20. "Sam Jones, A New Biography" (The Old Paths Publications: www.theoldpathspublications.com)

21. E. A. Johnston's Book Set, (The Old Paths Publications, www.theoldpathspublications.com (30% off retail)

22. "Revival Trilogy, Three Volumes in One": 1. "Realities of Revival," 2. "Call to Revival," 3. "The Church in Revival," The Old Paths Publications, Inc., www.theoldpathspublications.com

23.   "How to Have a Dailey Quiet Time," the Old Paths Publications, Inc.,
        www.theoldpathspublications.com
24.   "Going Higher With God," The Old Paths Publications, Inc.,
        www.theoldpathspublications.com
25.   "How to Preach For Revival," The Old Paths Publications, Inc.,
        www.theoldpathspublications.com
26.   "Faith Lessons in A Dynamic God," The Old Paths Publications, Inc.,
        www.theoldpathspublications.com

Many of these books can be purchased in The Old Paths Publications Bookstore at a discounted price and where you will find "Sample Pages." Go here:

https://www.theoldpathspublications.com/Pages/BookStore.htm